205.1, 34

AF805025

This book is due for return on or before the last date shown below.

Don Gresswell Ltd., London, N.21 Cat. No. 1208

DG 02242/71

PEM: 100375
AUT/ED: Morris, Johnathan
TITLE : Working for the Ja
CLASS : 205.1,34
COPY : 1

PEMBROKE COLLEGE
WITHDRAWN FROM LIBRARY
CAMBRIDGE

Working for the Japanese

Working for the Japanese

The Economic and Social Consequences of Japanese Investment in Wales

Jonathan Morris, Max Munday and Barry Wilkinson

PEMBROKE COLLEGE CAMBRIDGE

THE ATHLONE PRESS
London and Atlantic Highlands, NJ

First published 1993 by The Athlone Press
1 Park Drive, London NW11 7SG and
165 First Avenue, Atlantic Highlands, NJ 07716

© Max Munday, Jonathan Morris, Barry Wilkinson, 1993

British Library Cataloguing in Publication Data
A catalogue record for this book is available from the British Library

ISBN 0-485-11438-0

Library of Congress Cataloging in Publication Data

Morris, Jonathan, 1958–
Working for the Japanese: the economic and social consequences of Japanese investment in Wales / Jon Morris, Max Munday and Barry Wilkinson.
p. cm.
Includes bibliographical references and index.
ISBN 0-485-11438-0: $65.00
1. Investments, Japanese—Wales. 2. Wales—Economic conditions. 3. Wales—Social conditions. I. Munday, Max, 1962– . II. Wilkinson, Barry, 1956– . III. Title.
HG5443.W35M67 1993
332.6′73520429—dc20 93-1456i
CIP

All rights reserved. No part of this publication may be reproduced, stored in a retrieval system, or transmitted in any form or by any means, electronic, mechanical, photocopying or otherwise, without prior permission in writing from the publisher.

Typeset by Blackpool Typesetting Services Limited, Blackpool
Printed and bound in Great Britain by Bookcraft (Bath) Ltd.,

For Sophie, Nathan and Lily

Contents

List of Tables

List of Figures

Acknowledgements

A large proportion of the research for this book would have been impossible without the sponsorship of the Welsh Development Agency. We would also like to thank those Japanese and local managers within the manufacturing plants who gave up a great deal of their time during the spring of 1992 to be interviewed, and to provide data relevant to our project.

Although the bulk of the empirical material presented in this volume derives from our 1992 study of Japanese manufacturing investment in Wales, the questions we asked, and therefore the resulting analyses, are in part a result of our collaborative work with other members of the Cardiff Business School over the last few years. In this regard we would particularly like to thank Nick Oliver, Steve Hill and Graham Sewell, although obviously any errors or omissions are our own responsibility.

Koichi Ogasawara of Yamagata University, Japan, was Visiting Professor at Cardiff Business School during the most important period of study during 1992. Professor Ogasawara aided us in the research design and interviewing, and contributed to the interpretation of our findings. We would also thank Professor Douglas Anthony, Mrs Rosemary Smith and Miss Julie Ridge of the Centre for Japanese Studies, and Miss Trixi Greenhough of the Welsh Office 'Japanese in Schools' programme for guidance in the research work. Mrs Mair Price and Miss Karen Trigg provided much appreciated secretarial support throughout the study and during the writing of this book.

Introduction

The attraction of foreign manufacturing industry to disadvantaged areas has long been an important element of both national and EC regional policy. Throughout much of the recent past the bulk of incoming manufacturing investment entering the EC originated from North America. During the late 1970s and 1980s, however, Japan has become an increasingly important source of new manufacturing investment in the EC.

In the context of a regional development strategy it is hoped that foreign inward investment from Japan will provide employment, opportunities for local enterprise, incomes, and perhaps new technology and ideas. The role of Japanese multinational enterprise, in particular, in meeting the needs of regions has been the topic of prolonged debate. However, evidence that charts the full impact of Japanese manufacturing investment upon small host areas has been either limited or largely anecdotal. The purpose of this book is to provide an accurate appraisal of the economic, social and cultural impact of a high concentration of Japanese manufacturing investment in one EC area, Wales.

Japanese manufacturing industry has been present in Wales for just over two decades, but real growth in the level of investment and associated employment only occurred during the latter half of the 1980s. At 1991, 29 Japanese manufacturing units in Wales employed nearly 12,000 people or around 18 per cent of the employment created by overseas manufacturing. This proportion is continuing to grow, and evidence presented in this volume suggests that, even without any further announcement of new investments, by 1995 employment created by Japanese firms in Wales will increase to around 17,000 people. Thus Wales provides fertile ground for a study considering the full regional impact of Japanese investment.

The empirical findings presented here are in large part the result of an extensive study carried out by the authors in conjunction with the Welsh Development Agency during the spring of 1992. During the survey period the authors were able to complete over 80 interviews with staff in 23 Japanese manufacturing enterprises, the remaining firms being covered with questionnaires. The research was comprehensive and examined the present state of the enterprises, their operations, work organization and industrial relations, as well as their local trading and community linkages. As well as conducting interviews, we were able to observe factory operations at first hand, and we were provided with a whole range of documentation - more or less extensive in different companies - from supplier lists to collective agreements. Hence our data are both qualitatively and quantitatively rich. Where we have used data from this study in tabular form we have simply indicated 'Authors' Survey 1992'. In these cases *N* indicates the number of companies from which we gathered that specific information.

The plan of the book is as follows. Chapter 1 essentially provides a background and examines the factors that have influenced Japanese manufacturing investment within the EC. Chapter 2 provides a descriptive appraisal of the level and nature of Japanese manufacturing in Wales as at 1992. These introductory chapters are followed by five chapters which assess the economic, social and cultural impact of the Japanese plants. Chapter 3 examines both the direct and indirect economic impact of Japanese plants upon the Welsh economy. The Japanese presence is set within the economic needs of the local economy before its contribution in terms of job creation are assessed. The chapter goes on to consider the underlying quality of Japanese investment by considering the quality of employment creation, local purchasing linkages, the nature of plant operations, and the level of subsidiary autonomy.

Chapters 4 and 5 consider the social impact of Japanese firms at the organizational level. Chapter 4 examines work organization within Japanese subsidiaries and the experiences of local workforces working within the Japanese plants. Chapter 5 considers the personnel management practices of the subsidiaries which underpin the radically new work practices established by the Japanese.

In Chapter 6 we look at how trade unions in Wales have responded to the highly controversial industrial relations systems brought by the Japanese to Wales, and at the nature and role of trade unionism in the transplants.

Chapter 7 considers the 'corporate citizen' role of Japanese enterprise by examining linkages in the local Welsh communities. This includes an examination of the experiences of Japanese personnel in Wales. The second section of Chapter 7 considers the growing social and cultural linkages that are developing between Wales and Japan, and the extent to which the presence of Japanese enterprise has stimulated these linkages.

It is hoped to show within this volume that any consideration of the local impact of Japanese manufacturing investment must take into account a multitude of factors. Whilst some economic factors are readily quantifiable, there are other areas of social and cultural impact which are immeasurable but equally important within a process of regional development. A great deal of time, effort and finance has been used in bringing Japanese investment to Wales. Only an appreciation of the full scope of the local impact will show whether this effort has been justified, and whether future policy needs amendment to improve the contribution of Japanese investment to the local economy.

Foreword by the Rt Hon The Lord Walker of Worcester MBE PC

If, at the beginning of 1988, as the then Secretary of State for Wales I had promised that in the next five years Wales would obtain well over £4 billion in inward investment no one would have contemplated that that was possible. Wales, with a population of about 5% of the United Kingdom, has in recent years consistently obtained a massive share of all inward investment into Britain. Of the £4½ billion invested between 1988 and 1992 nearly £3½ billion came from overseas, and £743 million from the rest of Britain.

If, in proportion to the population, the rest of the UK had done as well as Wales, in those five years we would have obtained more than £70 billion of inward investment from overseas, an investment that would have transformed the British economy.

This book gives but some of the detail of the benefits that have been obtained. Due to no fault of the authors other benefits cannot be accurately measured: the creation of transport facilities to move the enormously increased exports from Wales that have been created by these new industries; the impact upon developments of the building industry in Wales that the building of these many new factories and offices has required; the extension of basic services of gas and electricity and water that has taken place; perhaps above all for the future the diversity of educational and training requirements that has been provided and the diversity of opportunity that now exists in the Principality.

The coal industry has almost disappeared. The steel industry is now substantial but modern and with a very much lower number of employees involved. The coal industry was never a kind industry to Wales. It polluted and above all it created a great deal of injury and ill health and it was an industry in constant decline for sixty years.

Many of the new activities will not be in decline but will be expanding industries of the future.

No longer is the only prospect for the children in the Valleys to go down a mine or else to become sufficiently academically qualified to become a teacher or a preacher. Now there is an ever-increasing dimension of opportunity and instead of the bright from Wales leaving for England and abroad quite a lot of the bright who left are returning.

Wales now also has an international connection that it had never previously enjoyed other than as a coal exporter. In the last five years Europe, North America and the Far East have all made a multitude of investments in the Principality. Many of the major investments will be followed by component suppliers from throughout the world establishing in Wales.

There are those who, as Europe entered recession and Japan met some fundamental economic problems, predicted that the flow would end and the coming years would be more difficult.

This is not the case. David Hunt showed that through the recession the flow of investments continued when in 1992 there were 206 new projects – four a week – bringing nearly £1 billion of new investment.

In 1993 we have seen some staggering expansions of overseas investment previously made: Bosch closing its Stuttgart factory to put more into Wales; a major Hong Kong company creating 1,000 new jobs: a Japanese company expanding its facilities with 500 further jobs.

The connections already established will be connections that will bring further investment to Wales in the years ahead.

This has been achieved by creating a team spirit in Wales.

The Welsh Development Agency has been outstanding. It has been vigorously led by Gwyn Jones, a young Welshman born in North Wales who has built up a business in South Wales, is a fluent speaker of the Welsh language and a man who has devoted four years of his life touring the world to bring business to Wales.

The local authorities who eagerly collaborated with me when I was Secretary of State so that they could encourage and bring all their services to the new investors.

Trade union leaders who, when required, provided single union agreement designed to improve productivity.

The businessmen in Wales who welcomed the new investors and provided them with the buildings and components that they required.

It has been a team effort of government, local authorities, trade unions and businessmen. It has been an example envied by the world at large.

ONE

Japanese Investment in Wales: The Backcloth

The theme of this book is a comprehensive analysis of Japanese investment in one, albeit key, European region from a variety of disciplinary perspectives, including applied economics, geography, industrial relations and organizational sociology. Notwithstanding this micro focus, the dramatic growth of such investment cannot be understood without reference to wider changes in the global economic order and the pivotal role that Japanese investment has played within this in the past decade.

Key features, for example, would be a rapid increase in the internationalization of capital generally and, more specifically, Japanese capital in the past two decades, the emergence of supranational markets at a world stage and a significant policy and corporate shift from an essentially trade based approach to international business relations to a capital-export, investment, approach on the part of Japan.

The essence, therefore the aim, of this chapter is to provide a backcloth to developments in Wales, thus including historical trends in Japanese investment, current trends and the patterns that have emerged at various scales, global, European and UK, in order to put developments in Wales into some perspective. The chapter will also offer some analysis of why these developments have occurred.

Historical trends of Japanese investment

In identifying trends of Japanese foreign direct investment (FDI) Dicken's schema is useful in periodizing the investment process.[1]

As Dicken argues, Japanese trade and investment policy in large part has been mercantilist, based on trade rather than on direct investment *per se*. However, this situation has clearly altered in the past ten to twenty years, as has the nature, sectoral composition and destination of the investment flows. Nevertheless, as a percentage of domestic production, in 1988 overseas production of Japanese companies was half of that of Germany, and a quarter that of the USA.[2]

Dicken outlines three major post-war phases. In the first, from 1945 to 1971, he notes modest growth rates before a considerable increase in the second phase, between 1971 and 1980. Finally, since 1985, he notes a steep upward trend. However, as was argued earlier, there have been considerable temporal variations in the destination of the investment flows. North America and Asia have received the bulk of the investment flows, with North America receiving the major share up until 1974, when it was overtaken by Asia before recovering the number one position in the 1980s, when there was major investment in transplants in North America across all industrial sectors, but especially in automobiles and electronics. Japanese investment in Europe meanwhile accelerated sharply after 1983 from a relatively small base, again associated with major investments in transplants – initially electronics but later automobiles. Dicken also notes considerable sectoral variations with investment in the earlier years biased considerably towards resource based sectors (notably mining). By the mid-1980s, however, there had been a considerable shift, with services (notably banking) the main recipient, followed by manufacturing, and resource-based industries relegated to third position. This sectoral composition also, however, varies geographically, with investment far more likely to be in services in North America and Europe, especially in the latter, than is the case in Asia, where sectoral patterns are more evenly spread, despite rapid increases in manufacturing investment in Asia in the 1980s.

Morris-Suzuki complicated this picture even further in arguing that the motives, and thus the nature, of manufacturing investment activity differ between Asia on the one hand and North America and Europe on the other.[3] In the latter, the investments tend to be stand alone and market orientated. In the former, however, and particularly the South-east and East Asian newly industrializing countries (NICs), the pattern is more complex. Initially manufacturing investment in these countries was concentrated in either heavy industries, such as metal manufacturing and chemicals, or relatively low-technology, labour-intensive industries such as textiles. However, there has been a large increase in activity in electronics and electronic components. This provides an international division of labour and production between Japan and those countries, with large Japanese corporations relocating parts of their model ranges, and especially lower-priced and value-added parts, to the NICs, which are then imported into Japan and exported elsewhere. Alternatively, electronic component production is being located in these NICs, again destined for the Japanese and other markets. Unlike the investments in North America and Europe, therefore, these are not primarily aimed at the domestic markets of the host countries but at an international market. Moreover, this production is also destined for the Japanese market, which explains a large increase in Japan–NIC manufacturing trade in the 1980s which, with notable exceptions, is not true of the North American and European transplants.

Dicken's periodization of Japanese FDI into three post-war phases has recently been extended by Ozawa.[4] Ozawa argues that a fourth phase has emerged, characterized by a profusion of technical alliances between Japanese, North American and European firms. Using data from the Japanese External Trade Organization (JETRO), he points to 48 alliances in the semi-conductor industry alone in 1990 between North American and Japanese manufacturers and European and Japanese manufacturers. This, Ozawa argues, is a result of Japan shifting from the third phase of industrialization and FDI, assembly based industrialization and the 'assembly transplanting' stage of multinationalism to what he terms 'A new era of flexible manufacturing and the "strategic localization/alliance" stage of global operations' (p.8). Of course, this represents the leading edge of FDI activity and much of the present activity in North America and Europe is more akin to the third phase.

Other authors, particularly in the business literature, have suggested slightly different explanations for patterns of Japanese investment. Ohmae, for example, views it in a wider perspective of the changing nature of international markets and the creation of a 'borderless world' in which national boundaries are disappearing.[5]

Others, while agreeing, have extended this analysis and have argued that, while national markets are becoming less important, they are to a certain extent being replaced by the emergence of three supranational markets, North America, Europe and Japan, South-east and East Asia.[6]

The three-, or triad-, market thesis would further argue that in order to adequately serve these markets, global multinational corporations need to transfer production to them; production here defined in the wider sense beyond mere manufacturing to involve research and development and a degree of management autonomy.

Later authors have argued in a similar vein inasmuch as the development of Japanese multinational corporations must be seen in a context of the changes in worldwide capitalism and not being driven by Japan *per se*.[7] This has echoes of an earlier, 1970s', debate which drew comparisons with the post-war patterns of US internationalization. In that debate certain authors were pointing to the uniqueness of Japanese internationalization.[8] Whereas US investment was based on more technologically advanced sectors, Japanese investment was not; and whereas US investment was in industrial sectors in which it held 'comparative advantage', Japanese investment was based on non-research-intensive industry with labour-intensive, technologically standardized products. Opponents of this view argued, however, that such deviations were relatively unimportant and that Japanese internationalization would evolve similar patterns to US investment.[9]

Emmott has partially resurrected this particular debate by arguing that, as is certainly the case with UK multinationals, Japanese multinationals will evolve irrespective of what happens to the Japanese economy, so that they will become less and less dependent upon that economy for markets and for production. Thus they will develop into truly global multinationals alongside US multinationals, such as IBM and General Motors.

Recent trends in Japanese FDI

The historical trends in Japanese FDI outlined above have continued in the past five years. Table 1.1, for example, illustrates that investment flows to North America continue to dominate, both in terms of the number of investments and total cumulative investment. Table 1.2 further illustrates this, with huge investment flows from Japan to North America in the years 1987 to 1991, and particularly in the years 1989 to 1990.

	Total 1990			*Cumulative total 1951–90*		
	No. of cases	*Amount ($)*	*%*	*No. of cases*	*Amount ($)*	*%*
North America	2,426	27,192	46.8	24,225	136,185	43.8
Latin America	339	3,628	6.4	7,197	40,483	13.0
Asia	1,499	7,054	12.4	18,634	47,519	15.3
Europe	956	14,294	25.1	7,425	59,265	19.1
Africa	70	551	2.0	1,458	5,826	1.9
Oceania	572	4,166	7.3	3,957	18,098	5.8

Table 1.1: *Japanese FDI by country, 1990, and cumulative total 1951–90*
Source: Japanese Ministry of Finance.

Elsewhere in the world, however, the picture has changed substantially. In terms of cumulative investment, for example, Europe had by 1991 overtaken Asia as the second largest single recipient, and this is also graphically illustrated by the data provided in Table 1.2, with Europe having far larger investment flows than Asia for all the years 1987 to 1991 and in certain years, 1990, for example, having twice the investment flow of Asia. Moreover, while the cumulative total of Japanese FDI in Asia was larger in 1990 than that for Latin America, in 1987 the Latin American total was greater than that for Asia.

The global sectoral breakdown of Japanese FDI for 1989 is indicated in Table 1.3. In Europe, manufacturing accounted for a much smaller percentage of total Japanese FDI than was the case in

Region	*1987*	*1988*	*1989 ($bn)*	*1990*	*1991*
Europe	6.6	9.0	14.8	14.3	9.4
North America	15.4	22.3	33.9	27.2	18.8
Asia	4.9	5.6	8.2	7.1	5.9
Latin America	4.8	6.4	5.2	3.6	3.3
Others	1.7	3.6	5.4	4.7	4.1
Total	33.4	47.0	67.5	56.9	41.5

Table 1.2: *Japanese FDI by world region, 1987–91*
Source: Japanese MITI.

	Total cumulative stock	Manufacturing 1989 ($bn)	%
Europe	44.972	7.947	17.7
North America	108.993	33.592	30.8
Asia	40.465	15.591	38.5
Latin America	36.855	5.633	15.3
Oceania	13.933	1.919	13.8
Africa	5.275	0.231	4.4
Middle East	3.404	1.276	37.5
Total	253.896	66.127	26.0

Table 1.3: *Japanese FDI in manufacturing by world region, 1989*
Source: INSEAD, Euro-Asian Centre.

North America or Asia, which follows historical trends. Moreover, the manufacturing percentage declined in the 1980s in Europe, whereas in Asia it was broadly similar, and in North America it increased slightly.

The pattern for the 1990s is likely to be that Japanese FDI in manufacturing will decline both globally, and more specifically in Europe, for two reasons. First, large Japanese companies are facing drastically reduced profits, and even losses in some cases, often for the first time in their post-war histories. Their response has been to dramatically downsize future investment projects and, although this may prove to be a short- to medium-term measure, it is unlikely that the flows of the 1980–90 decade will be repeated. Second, and probably more lasting, it is likely that the Japanese manufacturing investment boom in Europe in the 1980s was in part a product of specific market features, notably the unified EC market. Whilst Japanese manufacturing investment in Europe will continue in the 1990s, both through new facilities and, more particularly, through investments in existing facilities, a recent JETRO report indicates that already the pace of investment has begun to slow.[10]

Japanese FDI in Europe: country comparisons

The intra-European distribution of Japanese FDI is provided by Tables 1.4 and 1.5, which indicate that there are two major recipients of Japanese FDI, the UK and the Netherlands, followed by four more modest recipients: Belgium, Luxemburg, Germany

	Cumulative Japanese investment ($bn)		*Average annual rate of growth (%)*
	1980	*1990*	*1985–90*
UK	2.00	26.18	52.8
Belgium/Luxembourg	0.40	7.80	31.9
France	0.38	4.97	43.4
Germany	0.50	5.85	34.0
Ireland	0.15	0.72	22.5
Italy	0.67	1.22	46.7
Netherlands	0.30	14.77	54.3
Spain	0.17	2.24	34.3
Switzerland	0.19	2.55	31.0

Table 1.4: *Cumulative Japanese direct investment in selected European countries, 1980–90*
Source: US Department of Commerce, 1992.

and France. Of these, the UK dominates, both in terms of the number of investments and total investment. Moreover, as Table 1.5 also indicates, the UK increased its position in 1990 by taking a larger share of investment than its share of the accumulated total, as did the Netherlands, France and Germany.

	1987	*1988*	*1989 ($bn)*	*1990*	*1991*
UK	2.5	4.0	5.2	6.8	8.6
Netherlands	0.8	2.4	4.5	2.7	2.0
Luxembourg	1.8	0.7	0.7	0.2	0.3
Germany	0.4	0.4	1.1	1.2	1.1
France	0.3	0.5	1.1	1.3	0.8
Spain	0.3	0.2	0.5	0.3	0.4
Belgium	0.1	0.2	0.3	0.4	0.2
Ireland	0.1	0.0	0.1	0.1	0.1
Italy	0.1	0.1	0.3	0.2	0.3
Total	6.4	8.5	14.0	13.4	13.8

Table 1.5: *Japanese FDI in selected European countries, 1987–91*
Source: Japanese Ministry of International Trade and Industry.

Sector	%
Mining	2
Chemicals	2
General machinery	3
Transport machinery	4
Electrical machinery	7
Other manufacturing	6
Finance and insurance	40
Commerce	12
Real estate	12
Other services	6
Other	5

Table 1.6: *Cumulative Japanese FDI in Europe, 1991*
Source: Japanese Ministry of Finance.

The figures indicated in this table are, of course, total Japanese FDI and do not distinguish between sectors. The overall sectoral distribution is provided by Table 1.6. As we indicated earlier, Japanese FDI is far more concentrated in the service sector than in manufacturing. Within the service sector, finance/insurance is by far the most prominent sector (indeed, it is the predominant sector overall), with commercial real estate also important. Within manufacturing, two sectors dominate, electrical machinery (or electronics), and transport machinery (or automotive and related).

The sectoral distribution differs from country to country. In Luxembourg investment is, for example, almost totally service-sector related, while the service sector also dominates in other countries, such as the Netherlands. The countries with the largest Japanese-owned manufacturing sectors are the UK, France, Spain and Germany. Morris's 1989 survey gave some indication of the reasons for these countries being the most favoured within Europe.[11] Clearly, all are large markets, and have therefore been attractive to Japanese investors. The UK has been favoured for a number of reasons: the use of the English language, the positive attitude of successive governments, a lack of strong indigenous competition, and the availability of financial incentives. Germany's centrality to the European market has favoured it as a location, as has the level of worker skills, although the relatively high wages have been a disincentive to locate. France is also central to the European market geographically, although a major location factor has been that many of the Japanese investments there have been in the form of acquisition activity. The early investments in Spain were all home (Spanish) market orientated, as the Spanish market was heavily protected in its pre-EC years, and the only way to penetrate the market was by locating production facilities, in the form of joint ventures with Spanish companies. However, Spain has in the past five to ten years emerged as a low-wage location for Japanese investors.

Japanese manufacturing investment in the UK: a regional comparison

As the previous section illustrated, the late 1980s witnessed a dramatic increase in the number, scale and type of Japanese manufacturing operations within the UK. In 1983, Japanese manufacturing investment in the UK employed around 3,700 people, the bulk of these within manufacturers of consumer electronics goods. By 1989, 86 Japanese manufacturing establishments employed 27,000, again in electronics, but also in a range of other sectors, including automobiles, office automation equipment, chemicals and plastics, and construction equipment. In a relatively short time, as Table 1.7 indicates, Japanese manufacturing subsidiaries had overtaken German subsidiaries in terms of the numbers of employees, and were becoming a significant element of total UK manufacturing employment.

	1983		*1989*	
Source country	*No. employed*	*% total*	*No. employed*	*% total*
USA	459.5	62.4	395.0	54.5
France	31.3	4.3	41.2	5.7
Germany	24.0	3.3	24.6	3.4
Rest of EC	53.2	7.2	67.7	9.3
Japan	3.7	–	27.2	3.8
Others	164.3	22.3	168.4	23.3
Total	736.0	100.0	724.1	100.0

Table 1.7: *Employment in foreign-owned manufacturers in the UK, 1983 and 1989*
Source: Census of Production (UK), PA 1002.

This spectacular growth in employment continued into the 1990s; between 1990–1 and 1991–2 alone, a further 81 Japanese projects entered the UK, with an estimated (projected) employment of 11,500.[12] This new employment reflects not only new greenfield investments, but an increasing number of joint ventures, acquisitions and expansion of existing facilities. Total employment in Japanese manufacturing subsidiaries was around 51,000 in 1992, representing just over 1 per cent of UK manufacturing employment.

When Dunning made his initial 1986 survey into the Japanese manufacturing presence in the UK, he observed that there were two types of geographical concentration: the primary concentrations were found in the peripheral industrialized regions of the UK, namely Wales, Scotland and the North-east of England.[13] A secondary concentration was found in the new towns of South-east England and the West Midlands (Milton Keynes and Telford in particular). As Table 1.8 indicates, Japanese investment was far wider spread geographically in 1992 than six years earlier, with a presence in all of the UK standard planning regions. In terms of the number of plants, five regions dominate: the South-east, the North, Wales, Scotland and the West Midlands. This pattern is very similar to that in 1986, although there has been a considerable increase in Japanese plants in the West Midlands, due in large part

	No. of plants	*Employment*	*% UK total*
Northern	22	6,315	12.4
Yorks and Humberside	7	2,770	5.5
East Midlands	11	1,808	3.6
East Anglia	9	1,548	3.0
Southern	37	6,225	12.3
South-west	7	1,749	3.4
West Midlands	24	8,443	16.6
North-west	19	2,434	4.8
Wales	31	13,024	25.6
Scotland	24	5,162	10.2
Northern Ireland	3	1,325	2.6
UK Total	194	50,803	100.0

Table 1.8: *UK regional distribution of Japanese-owned plants and employment, 1992*
Source: Anglo-Japanese Journal, 6 (1), May 1992.

to the growth of Japanese automotive component transplants, a combination of, mainly, acquisition activity and joint ventures, but also greenfield activity. The regions differ in their sectoral profile – Wales and Scotland, for example, have a strong electronics presence. In Northern England and the West Midlands, however, the profile is more focused upon engineering and auto components, unsurprising given the presence of the Nissan plant in the former and the fact that the latter is the traditional heartland of the auto and auto components sector.

Previous studies have given reasons for the location decisions of Japanese manufacturers in the various UK regions.[14] However, these initial concentrations have tended to be reinforced in two ways. First, early and important locators such as Sony in Wales and Nissan in the North-east have provided a dynamic in that other original equipment manufacturers in the same or similar sectors have followed them. Second, component manufacturers have understandably tended to locate in these regions, as the next chapter will illustrate, with electronics components in the Welsh case and automotive/engineering components in the North-east.

Conclusions

What will emerge from the remainder of this book is that the Japanese manufacturing presence in Wales has increased dramatically in the past decade, that this has far reaching economic consequences on the Welsh economy and that, both directly and indirectly, this Japanese investment has, in varying degrees, transformed work organization, industrial relations and personnel management in Wales.

Such developments, however, have to be set in a wider context of a rapid internationalization dash by the major Japanese industrial corporations, encouraged by government in a quick about-turn in policy, forced by rapid adverse currency movements and encouraged by the changing nature of global markets and political structures.

The remainder of the book is divided broadly into various disciplinary perspectives. The next two chapters, for example, have a broadly applied economics focus: Chapter 2 concentrates on the plant level, and Chapter 3 reviews some of the wider economic and economic policy implications. Chapters 4, 5 and 6 concentrate on what might be termed human resource management issues: the organization of work, personnel management and industrial relations. Finally, Chapter 7 discusses the wider social impact of this Japanese investment, its impact on the community and its effect on Japanese personnel in Wales.

Two

Japanese Investment in Wales: The Who, Why and What

When the Japanese firm, Takiron, located a plant at Bedwas in the Rhymney Valley in 1972, few could have predicted the scale and nature of Japanese industry's involvement in the Welsh economy in the 1990s. Takiron was a relatively minor investment from a relatively small and unknown firm. Twenty years later many of Japan's blue chip companies are located in the country – Toyota, Sony, Matsushita, Sharp, etc. – as part of a total of 44 investments involving 31 manufacturing concerns.

This study is not the first survey of Japanese investors in Wales. In the mid-1980s there were three major studies. In 1986 Arthur D. Little conducted a study on behalf of the Welsh Development Agency which, despite yielding useful information, was essentially a promotional exercise for the group. A year later Munday made a far more extensive and scholarly study of Japan's investment in Wales and Morris reported, controversially, Japanese investment in Wales as part of a wider EEC study.[1]

Despite these studies only being five or six years old, a new study is timely, due to the growth of investment over that period. At the time of the Arthur D. Little study, for example, there were only 11 Japanese plants in Wales and only one had been added a year later. Moreover, as this chapter will explain, it is not only the number of plants which have increased, nor the employment and investment totals, but the nature of these investments has changed in a number of respects as the plants have matured and become embedded in the Welsh, UK and European economies.

This chapter will open with a description of empirical data, outlining the companies which have located, why they have located, what they have located, how many people they employ, what is the nature of the employment, how much is invested, etc. Essentially, then, it is a backcloth to the more focused issues in later chapters of the book such as the wider economic impact, industrial relations issues, work organization, buyer supplier relations and community linkages.

The remainder of this chapter is divided into five sections. The next section will outline what companies have come to Wales, when they came, in what industrial sectors they are found and what markets they serve. Following on from this will be a section on employment creation and then a section on the economic performance of the plants. The penultimate section will describe the different types of plant operation in Wales, and the final section will deal with the plant location decisions.

The companies and their markets

At the time of the study there were 42 Japanese investments in Wales which, at a general level, can be divided into manufacturing facilities on the one hand, and a group of sales, distribution and miscellaneous activities on the other. Manufacturing facilities predominate, with 29 operations (see Table 2.1, across). Moreover, while the latter group are important (Table 2.2) they are small employers; none employs more than 20 in comparison with the large numbers employed in the manufacturers (see Table 2.3). In 1992 this total swelled to 44 facilities when the Toyota engine plant at Shotton (North Wales) and Kasai Kogyo, an auto components facility at Merthyr, began production. While this book will address the wider aspects of Japanese involvement in Wales, the prime focus will be upon these 29 manufacturing concerns. For 'Japanese-owned' we adopted a flexible interpretation including facilities with a major Japanese involvement, which we regarded as a 'Japanese investment'. In the majority of cases this was irrelevant; 18 out of the 26 cases studied were 100 per cent owned subsidiaries of their parent companies, of the remaining 8 firms on which we had access to information, 5 were majority Japanese-owned joint ventures, with 3 UK-Japanese joint ventures (see Table 2.1).

The question of 'additionality' is, of course, a complex one. Do foreign direct investments, for example, provide 'extra' employment

Company	*Parent*	*Location*	*Established*
Aiwa	Aiwa	Crumlin, Gwent	1980
Brother Industries	Brother	Wrexham	1985
Calsonic	Calsonic	Llanelli	1989
Diaplastics	Mitsubishi Trading; Mitsubishi Plastics	Bridgend	1988
Dowty–Koike	Dowty; Koike Rubber	Wrexham	1991
Dynic	Dynic	Cardiff	1989
Electronic Harnesses	Onamba; Sumitomo Electric	Llantrisant, Mid Glam	1988
GKK	Japan Plastics; Brother	Wrexham	1989
Gooding–Sanken	Gooding Group; Sanken	Aberdare, Mid Glam	1990
Hitachi	Hitachi	Aberdare, Mid Glam	1979
Hoya Lens	Hoya	Wrexham	1980
Kasai Kogyo	Not available	Merthyr Tydfil	1992
Kyushu Matsushita Electric	Matsushita Electric	Newport	1986
Kyushu Matsushita Electric Information System	Not available	Cwmbran	1989
Lucas–SEI	Lucas; Sumitomo Electric; Sumitomo Wiring	Swansea	1990
Matsushita Electric	Matsushita Electric	Cardiff	1976
Matsushita Electronic Components	Matsushita Electronic Components; Matsushita Electric	Port Talbot	1976
Matsushita Electronic Magnetron	Matsushita Electronic Magnetron	Cwmbran	1990
Meiki UK Ltd	Meiki, Mitsubishi	Bridgend	1989
Optec DD	Optec DD	Buckley, Clwyd	1987
Orion Electric	Orion	Port Talbot	1986
Sekisui	Sekisui	Merthyr Tydfil	1978
Sharp Manufg	Sharp	Wrexham	1985

Company	*Parent*	*Location*	*Established*
Sharp Precision	Sharp; Sharp Precision Machinery	Wrexham	1988
Sony	Sony	Bridgend	1973
Star Micronics	Star Micronics	Tredegar, Gwent	1988
Takiron	Takiron	Newport	1972
Toyota Motor	Toyota	Shotton, Clwyd	1992
Tsuda	Tsuda	Wrexham	1988
Yuasa Battery	Yuasa	Ebbw Vale	1982
Zeon Chemicals	Zeon	Barry	1989

Table 2.1: *Japanese manufacturing concerns in Wales, 1992: ownership, location and date of establishment*
Source: Authors' Survey, 1991.

Company	*Business*	*Location*	*Established*
Aoki Corporation	Property developers	Cardiff	1991
Kinetsu World Express	Freight forwarders warehousing, sales	Caerphilly Mid Glam	1990
Marubeni Komatsu	Import and distribution	Cwmbran	1967
Premiership Distribution	Warehousing, shipping and distribution	Newport	1990
Roland	Sales, marketing and distribution	Swansea	1990
Sanyo Oil	Sports and leisure	Monmouth	—
Sato Import and Export	Sales and distribution	Cardiff	1990
Shimano	Service and distribution	Swansea	1986
Sumitomo Electric	Sales, marketing and distribution	Port Talbot	1989
Taiko Electronics	Sales and marketing	Cwmbran	1988
Takenaka	Architects, planners builders and contractors	Cardiff	1981
Tomoe Saunders	Service and distribution	Newport	1986
Yamato Transport	Freight warehousing	Cardiff	1989

Table 2.2: *Japanese non-manufacturing concerns in Wales*
Source: Authors' Survey, 1992.

and investment? Clearly, at a superficial level greenfield investments provide this additionality. However, the impact upon indigenous producers needs to be considered: for example, are new greenfield investments replacing jobs in existing manufacturers? The impact of the Japanese colour television producers upon British manufacturers is a graphic illustration of this,[2] although it is arguable that the Japanese competition in this sector would have been severe from trading alone and that the location of Japanese producers at least saved and secured employment. The impact of 3 automotive producers on existing UK auto producers remains to be seen.

Nevertheless, the theme of this book, and one to which we will return in subsequent chapters, is that Japanese investment in Wales has had a major impact upon the Welsh economy, not only in terms of the number of plants and employment creation, but in its wider role in economic restructuring, broader impacts on the economy, the reshaping of the industrial relations agenda and the transfer of new forms of work organization.

In terms of product sectors, the investments were divided fairly evenly between electronics related activities and a broad group of other industries. The former included 16 investments and the latter 13, including plastics, chemicals and related, lenses and automotive components (Table 2.3). More specifically, the electronics grouping were again evenly divided between manufacture of consumer electronics products (6), office electronic equipment and related (4) and electrical and electronic components (6). The importance of the electronics investments is further emphasized by their size, at least in employment terms. The two largest employers are electronics investments, as are 7 of the top 10 largest Japanese employers in Wales (Table 2.3).

The investments were also fairly evenly split between those who produce on an original equipment manufacture basis (12) and those producing components and semi-finished products (17), although again the former group tended to be larger investments in both financial and employment terms. The component manufacturers also tended to be far more recent locators, supporting a 'two wave' thesis of Japanese investment in Wales; the first wave comprised almost solely of original equipment manufacturers (OEMs), and the second was dominated by components and parts manufacturers (Table 2.4). It also reflects changes in the investment process since

PEMBROKE COLLEGE CAMBRIDGE

Company	*Products*	*Employment*
Aiwa	Audio hi-fi systems	230
Brother Industries	Typewriters, dot matrix printers, microwave ovens	500
Calsonic	Automotive heat exchangers	820
Diaplastics	Plastic covers, panels and components	185
Dowty–Koike	Polymeric components	74
Dynic	Computer printer ribbons	25 (E)
Electronic Harnesses	Electronic harnesses	106
GKK Plastics	Plastic injection mouldings	60
Gooding–Sanken	Transformers	220
Hitachi	Colour televisions, videocassette recorders, microwave ovens	850
Hoya Lens	Spectacle lenses	104
Kyushu Matsushita Electric	Electronic typewriters and Electric printers	554 (E)
Kyushu Matsushita EIS	PABX manufacture Electric Information Systems	154 (E)
Lucas-SEI	Automative wiring systems	1,447
Matsushita Electric	Colour televisions, microwave ovens	2,000
Matsushita Electronic Components	Transformers and filters	179
Matsushita Electronic Magnetron	Magnetrons	26
Meiki UK Ltd	Pressure injection plastic moulds	15
Optec DD	Wire harnesses and copper magnet wire	154
Orion Electric	Colour televisions and video cassette recorders	410
Sekisui	Polyethylene and polypropylene foam	80
Sharp	Video cassette recorders, electronic typewriters, copiers, compact disc players, microwave ovens	1,040
Sharp Precision	Precision metal pressings	92
Sony	Colour television, monitors, tubes and components	2,500
Star Micronics	Dot matrix printers	340
Takiron	PVC corrugated sheeting	95
Tsuda	Plastic injection mouldings	108
Yuasa Battery	Batteries	560
Zeon Chemicals	Speciality synthetic rubber and lattices	85

Table 2.3: *Japanese manufacturing concerns in Wales: products and employment*
Source: Authors' Survey, 1992.

Note: E = estimate.

Date of location	*No. of plants*	*OEMs*	*Components, sub-assemblies, semi-finished*
Pre-1980	5	4	1
1980–4	3	3	0
1985–9	17	5	12
1990–2	4	0	4

Table 2.4: *Date of location of Japanese plants in Wales by OEMs and others*
Source: Authors' Survey, 1992.

since the earlier, but nevertheless fairly recent, surveys of Japanese investment in Wales and on a broader UK stage.[3]

The majority of the plants produced a single product range (17), although 7 produced two types of products, 4 produced three, and 1 produced four. This, however, tends to understate the diversity of these investments for three reasons. First, the 'single-product group' is dominated by the component manufacturers, which tend to specialize in one component but which produce a wide variety. Secondly, within this group there are OEM producers with very broad ranges of single products plus substantial component manufacture. Thirdly, the definition is in itself somewhat restrictive as a car manufacturer could be said to belong to a 'single product group', yet have a substantially complex product range.

The increasing product diversity contrasts again with earlier studies which indicated single product manufacture, and is a reflection of the evolution of these plants, which in many instances are fairly new. If we compare Munday's (1990) study, for example, with Table 2.3, we find that most of the large electronics groups have added to their product range in the ensuing five years: Sharp, for example, added compact disc player and photocopier production to its existing two products. Moreover, nearly one-half (11) of the respondents replied to the question on new product additions that further new products were already being introduced or were at a firm planning stage, while 3 respondents were unsure and 10 replied no. These results are set in a context of the UK and EEC economies being in recession with considerable business uncertainty.

As was mentioned earlier, the plants were divided into two broad waves in terms of start up. The first started in 1972 when Takiron located and there was continual steady investment through to the end of 1980 when there were 7 Japanese manufacturing plants in Wales. In the first half of the 1980s there were few investors (only one between 1980 and 1985), but investment started picking up again in the late 1980s, with 1988 (6 locations), 1989 (5) and 1990 (4) being particularly strong years. The last years of this second wave were characterized, and dominated, by the location of component suppliers; only one of the investments made in these years was by an OEM (see Table 2.4).

This 'second wave' of component suppliers reflects both a growing maturity of Japanese investment in the UK and the necessity to increase local content sourcing.[4] The majority of component suppliers are those connected to the electronics industry. Seven of the 17 non-OEM manufacturers are in the electronics field, with 7 in plastics, chemicals and rubber, and 3 automotive component and related manufacturers. In reality, however, 12 of these manufacturers are supplying directly to the electronics OEMs. Although supplier firms were sometimes dependent on one major customer, most had a diversified supply base. Of the 12 firms that provided information on this question, 3 had two customers, 3 had three, 3 had four customers, 1 had five and 2 firms had six customers.

A growing maturity of investment is also reflected in the number of plants each Japanese company has in Wales, the UK and the wider EEC. Two parent companies had more than one operation in Wales: Matsushita have five operations (two as Kyushu Matsushita) and Sharp two. In addition, Brother have a part ownership in a supplier, GKK. Of the 19 companies from which information was available, the majority (11) had no other plant in the EEC. Of the 8 remaining, half had plants which competed to a certain extent with the Welsh plant, while the other half had sister plants which either produced unrelated products or which did not compete directly.

A number of the Japanese companies in Wales, then, have networks of plants throughout the EEC, often which work within a complementary division of labour. In some cases these are relatively simple; Brother, for example, has a plant in Ireland which supplies its North Wales plants with printed circuit boards. In other cases the plants produce differing products; Calsonic, for example, has four other EEC plants (two in North-east England, two in Continental Europe) producing different types of automotive components. In yet other cases, the plants produce broadly similar products; Hoya Lens, for example, has five similar European plants due to the peculiarities and specificities of this particular product market.

Perhaps the best examples of integrated production facilities are those of Matsushita and Sony. Matsushita, for example, as we have already seen, has five plants in Wales, with two component factories supplying to the main OEM production facility. Sony, meanwhile, has eight European plants producing a variety of consumer electronics products and accessories. The Sony Bridgend plant supplies the two other colour television plants at Barcelona and Stuttgart, which produce different CTV models, with tubes and other key components.

The Japanese plants in Wales are also integrated to a certain extent in market orientation (see Table 2.5). Only 3 of the 24 respondent companies did not export; all 3 were component producers and were fairly recent investors (the oldest was 1987). Meanwhile, 11 of the plants exported over 50 per cent of their output, including two cases of over 75 per cent. Moreover, 18 of the 24 anticipated a growth in exports, including the 3 plants which did not as yet export. The degree of market orientation and export ratios is perhaps not surprising given the internationalization of markets to a pan European scale. However, given the number of plants which are essentially suppliers and subcontractors and which initially followed Japanese OEM investment to Wales and the UK, these figures emphasize this export orientation.

% exported	*No. of plants*
0	3
>10	2
10–24	8
25–49	0
50–74	9
75+	2

Table 2.5: *Percentage of output exported from Japanese plants in Wales*
Source: Authors' Survey, 1992.

Export markets tended to be exclusively European, either EEC or, more generally, the wider EFTA net; only 2 firms exported outside Europe, both small amounts, to North Africa and the Middle East, respectively. In only 3 cases was there any split definition of market territory. In the vast majority of cases of course, either the Welsh plant was the only EEC plant or other plants produced different products.

Employment

Total employment at 27 of the 29 plants surveyed was 13,024 (this included two informed estimates). In the two remaining plants employment is likely to be no more than 200, giving a total of approximately 13,200. Informed estimates for the non-manufacturing concerns suggest that total employment in these companies is not likely to exceed 150.

The rapid growth of Japanese investment in Wales is illustrated by reference to previous studies. Dunning's (1986) study, for example, indicated that Japanese companies in the whole of the UK only employed 11,200 at 45 plants, while the 1986 Arthur D. Little survey pointed to 3,789 employees in Wales.[5] Average plant size was therefore approximately 483. Table 2.6 indicates the various plant sizes. In general, there was a close relation between ages of plants and number of employees; the 2 plants with over 2,000 employees, for example, located in 1973 and 1976 respectively, although there were old but relatively small plants. Component suppliers tended to employ fewer people (although one automotive

Employees	*No. of plants*
Under 100	8
100–199	6
200–399	2
400–599	5
600–799	0
800–999	2
Over 1000	4

Table 2.6: *Employment size of Japanese plants in Wales*
Source: Authors' Survey, 1992.

component supplier employed nearly 1,500). Finally, as we have already indicated, the electronics investments were amongst the largest, in employment terms.

The employment total of approximately 13,200 is likely to grow considerably in the short term, according to the future employment projections of firms. Of the 22 responses to this question, 16 reported that there would be an expansion of employment within the next three years, 5 responded that employment levels would remain static, and 1 (a take-over) reported that employment levels would fall. These findings are perhaps unremarkable given that many plants are relatively new and building up capacity, but are encouraging given the parlous state of the UK and wider world economy at the time of this survey.

Of the 16 firms reporting future employment expansion, 10 actually specified the number of new jobs which would be created, with a total number of new jobs of 3,510. Two major and well publicized expansions account for over half of this new job creation: Lucas–SEI announced that it was employing 500 new workers shortly after our interview, and Sony's new plant near Bridgend will increase this company's employment in Wales from 2,500 to 4,000. In addition, of course, the new Toyota engine plant in North Wales will employ 300, with the likely result that by the mid-1990s, barring a worsening of the economic climate, Japanese firms in Wales will employ well over 17,000. Moreover, the interviews took place between January and April, a part of the year when Japanese plants – particularly in consumer electronics – employ far fewer people than later in the year. It should be noted, however, that 6 of the companies had recently cut employment levels either through natural wastage or non-retention of temporary staff. Only one of these firms had, however, made compulsory redundancies.

Whilst Japanese companies are employing substantial numbers of workers in Wales, the question remains of what type of employment they are creating. There have been substantial criticisms in the past that such plants were exploiting the large labour surplus in Wales to create a largely female, low-skilled workforce, whereas the overwhelming need – given male job loss in the coal and steel industries – was for male skilled jobs.[6] This survey is not directly comparable to the earlier surveys, and in particular the critical Morris article.[7] Firms were asked, for example, what percentage of their workforce were male and female, but this was a plant-level breakdown, whereas the earlier Morris survey concentrated upon production workers. Moreover, this study made no attempt to categorize the skill levels of workers, for the simple reason that we felt that this was such a difficult task that it would be a meaningless, if not misleading, exercise. However, several of the questions, notably on research capability in this chapter, and on training provisions in a later chapter, perhaps give a wider flavour of the nature of job creation in these plants.

In the 24 plants for which data was available, 5,803 males were employed, compared to 7,153 females. Those plants in which there were mainly males employed outnumbered those where females dominated (11 to 10, with 3 employing roughly equal numbers). However, obviously the former tended to be smaller on average in employment terms.

Compared to previous surveys, therefore, and in particular the Arthur D. Little study, the number of females as a percentage of the total workforce has actually increased. There are a number of possible reasons for this. First, while the number of new firms – since the Little survey – employing a majority male workforce is equal to that with a mainly female workforce, the latter group have, in most cases, much larger workforces. In particular, in one of the post-Little survey locaters, which is the third largest Japanese employer in Wales, female employees outnumber male employees by a ratio of 6 to 1. Second, the firms which have expanded their employment most rapidly since the Little survey tend to be employers of a large proportion of females. However, in certain instances firms are employing a lower percentage of female workers, as new products, processes and functions have been added.

In the 22 firms for which data was available, 1,578 managers and/or salaried staff were employed, compared to 9,277 other grades. The percentage of managers tended to be higher in smaller plants and in plants with relatively capital intensive production processes. However, there were plants with large numbers of managers in industries with relatively labour-intensive production processes. In one of the largest employers, for example, a CTV producer, 20 per cent of employees were in non-production grades. This is a clear indication that the nature of some of these plants is changing. That is, the plants are developing away from the assembly-only stereotype and are employing, in some cases, large numbers of managers and engineers. This is confirmed to a certain extent by comparing this survey to the earlier Little survey. In that study 10.8 per cent of total employees were in managerial grades. Given the growth of individual plant workforces, it might have been expected that the percentage of managers would have declined. On the contrary, however, the percentage of managers overall has actually increased to 17 per cent. Moreover, in the firms for which comparable data are available for the Little survey and this survey, the percentage of managers has increased in all but one, the exception being a relatively small employer.

This observation is confirmed to a certain extent by the answers to the next question: how many graduates do you employ? In the 24 firms responding to this question, 542 graduates were employed out of a total of 12,217 employees. While this overall percentage is relatively low at 4.6 per cent, the figures for certain plants were substantially higher. In one of the larger consumer electronics concerns, for example, 8 per cent of total employees were graduates, indicating again a diversification from the assembly-type factory.

A total of 208 Japanese staff were employed out of 12,325 overall employees in the 24 firms responding to this question. Typically, Japanese staff are in managerial, technical and engineering functions, in some cases with 'shadow' managerial groups of indigenous managers. In one large electronics manufacturer, for example, the management team was comprised of a Japanese managing director, 3 Japanese co-directors, a British senior manager, 2 Japanese and three British general managers, 23 British and 12 Japanese managers and 18 British and 4 Japanese assistant managers. The percentage of Japanese managers to overall employees varies greatly between plants; one plant, for example, has no Japanese managers, while in another, 20 per cent of employees are Japanese (although this plant only employs 15). In general, however, the proportion of Japanese managers tends to be highest in smaller and/or newer plants, supporting the hypothesis that as plants mature, fewer Japanese managers are employed and are gradually replaced by indigenous managers. In one of the smaller newer plants, for example, the number of Japanese expatriates had declined from 11 to 4 in the past two years. The overall percentage of Japanese employees in this survey, for example, is markedly lower than in the Little survey.

The final employment question regarded recruitment difficulties: 23 of the firms responded to this question, although one of these was shedding labour and another had an existing workforce, and thus recruitment was not an issue in these cases. Of the remainder 12 reported recruitment difficulties, while 9 reported no problems. The large number in the former category might appear somewhat surprising, given the slack labour market conditions in Wales at a time of economic recession. However, the problems were found, not in the recruitment of labour *per se*, but in recruiting certain types of labour. One firm, for example, reported that 'at present we have 1,500 on our waiting list'. In 10 of the 12 cases firms reported difficulties in recruiting various types of engineering staff (particularly electronics engineers) and technicians. In the 2 other cases firms reported difficulties in recruiting toolmakers and quality control staff. Interestingly, however, one of the largest electronics producers reported no difficulties in staff recruitment due to an in-house apprentice scheme, which perhaps begs the question of why other of the firms did not provide such training infrastructure.

Economic performance

The survey asked four main questions which can be categorized under the umbrella of economic performance: turnover, profitability, capital investment and future investment intentions. As Table 2.7 indicates, turnover varied enormously, from £0.75 million in the case of the smallest investor, to approximately £400 million in the case of the largest. As the table also indicates, the majority of

£ Million	*Number*
>10	10
10–24	3
25–49	2
50–99	5
100–199	1
200–399	1
400+	1

Table 2.7: *Turnover of Japanese plants in Wales*
Source: Authors' Survey, 1992.

companies had a turnover of less than £100 million (20 of the 23 respondents), with 10 of these with turnovers of less than £10 million. These were primarily component producers which were generally recent locators. It should be noted, however, that many plants were selling to in-company sales organizations and that these figures do not necessarily reflect market values.

As to the question of profitability, 22 firms responded. Of these 13 reported that they were in a profit situation, 4 reported a break-even situation, and 5 reported that they were making a loss. Several plants were acting as cost centres. Again, this situation must be set within a context of very difficult trading conditions and economic recession at the time of the survey. Moreover, again it must be remembered that many of the firms are recent locators. Indeed, there was a close relationship between profitability and date of location with one of the loss making facilities locating in 1988, three in 1989 and one in 1991.

The last two questions were related to capital investment and future investment intentions. As Table 2.8 illustrates, the majority of firms had under £10 million invested (10 of 18 respondents). At the other end of the spectrum, however, there were two firms with £120 million investments. In terms of future investment decisions, 23 firms responded, with the majority (19) indicating that they had firm investment plans, including 8 reporting that they were currently implementing major capital-investment projects.

£ Million	*Number*
>10	10
10–19	4
20–49	2
50–99	—
100–149	2

Table 2.8: *Capital investment in Japanese plants in Wales*
Source: Authors' Survey, 1992.

Plant operations and productivity

Firms were asked to describe in a phrase their plant operations; were they mainly an assembly operation, manufacturing, process, etc., or a combination. Table 2.9 summarizes the main types of

Operation	*Number of plants*
Assembly	11
Assembly and manufacture	3
Assembly, manufacture and development	4
Manufacture and development	2
Manufacture	1
Process	4

Table 2.9: *Operations of Japanese plants in Wales*
Source: Authors' Survey, 1992.

operations. Assembly was the most popular form of operation, with 11 plants. What this represented was a production process which was involved with the assembly of bought-in parts: 3 firms were engaged in assembly and manufacture, the latter referring to the production of major components in house, while a further 4 firms were involved in these two activities plus development work. In addition 1 carried out only manufacture, and 2 manufacture plus development work. Finally, 4 firms were involved in process operations such as chemicals or plastics production.

It is worth dwelling perhaps on the nature of two of these activities, manufacture and development work, because they are part of a wider debate on the value of Japanese manufacturing investment activity. In the past, Japanese manufacturing plants have been criticized for being low-skill-based assembly operations with low value-added.[8] Indeed, one group of authors has characterized them as 'warehouses'.[9] Our study would not, however, support this conclusion. Our argument would be that Japanese investments in Wales may well have been of this type at one stage (although even Morris's controversial paper argued that in the 1980s not all investments were like this),[10] but that certain of these investments have matured and 'deepened' from assembly operations to manufacturing concerns and even added development work in some cases. Several of the plants had taken in-house component production which would be subcontracted out in Japan and previously had been in Wales, due to problems of delivery and quality.

Even our findings may understate this case, as 4 of the 11 plants characterized as assembly operations, for example, also carry out some manufacturing, such as printed circuit board production.

Moreover, nearly half of the plants (excluding the four process operations, which exhibit a very different production process) have extended well beyond this to manufacture.

Perhaps the best illustration of this process is the Sony colour television plant at Bridgend. Not only does the plant assemble colour televisions, but it produces the two key critical CTV components, picture tubes (over half of the value of the television) and deflector yokes. In addition, other sub-assemblies and components such as PCBs are produced in house. Indeed, this plant has been described as the most vertically integrated television plant in the world. Not all of the plants have such extensive manufacturing facilities as those at Sony, but many clearly have production processes which extended well beyond the assembly stage.

In a number of cases this extended further to research and development (R&D) work, development or design. Of the 25 firms that responded to the questions on R&D, 10 carried out some sort of design work. Several of the component suppliers offered a design capability to customers, although in others design was agreed between the parent and client in Japan. In three cases this was limited to rudimentary design work, but in others extensive development work was carried out. The largest R&D group, for example, comprised 80 employees, and two other plants had R&D departments with over 50 people. In addition, one further firm was starting the process of transfer of R&D activities to Wales. Whilst the precise nature of the work done in these facilities was not detailed, the very size of them suggests that they are not of the limited design/rebadging type. Indeed, the R&D department being developed at Sony will be the European CTV R&D centre. Fifty per cent of CTV development work will be undertaken at the centre, with the remaining basic research carried out in Japan. One of the other large consumer electronics producers had chosen Germany for its R&D centre, citing a lack of engineering talent in the UK.

The third question asked of respondents in this section related to productivity in relation to sister plants in Japan and/or sister transplants in other countries. This is, of course, an extremely tricky area, as plants differ in terms of capital intensity, amount subcontracted, etc. However, it was thought that even with these caveats some broad inferences could be drawn. The problems of productivity comparisons are reflected in the responses; 11 of the 24 firms found this question not applicable. This was for a variety of reasons; for example, either firms did not make productivity comparisons or plants were so different that they were rendered useless. In the remaining 13 cases, 5 respondents said that productivity was equal to Japanese sister plants and 8 replied that it was less. Of the 5 that ventured a reason for this, 2 mentioned that this was due to differing 'attitudes' of workers and 3 ascribed the differential to a 'learning curve' effect due to their plant's recent location. In relation to the former reason one (Japanese) respondent summed up the differences:

> In this country people behave naturally. In Japan they are forced to do it . . . they want to climb up to the higher position, so they work hard. Our headache is human management, because of differences in culture. Japanese people don't want to work at night any more though. And commonsense here is much better.

A second Japanese respondent in a different plant replied:

> [Compared with Japan, it's the] mentality of the Japanese people. There, when the buzzer goes off at 12 o'clock for lunch or 5 o'clock for shift end, they do the job until they've finished it. Here they stop. The attitude to work is different.

The final operational question asked of firms was how closely they were controlled from Japan. Again, of course, this is an extremely subjective question and one which is difficult to answer without using objective measures. One respondent, for example, replied 'like the others!'. Responses were fairly evenly split, with 8 replying that they were closely controlled and 9 not closely controlled. The latter included the joint ventures where the British partner would be expected to exert more influence than in a wholly owned subsidiary. One respondent, for example, described the plant as closely controlled from Japan:

> We are in daily contact by fax and telephone with Japan on a lot of subjects, including detailed financial information, factory plans and layouts. But I'm only guessing, I don't speak Japanese and only the Japanese managers communicate with Japan.

Another described a similar situation:

> It can be very centralized. Many small matters go back to Japan. If a letter is sent to the DTI this would normally be faxed back first . . . A change in product design would need approval from Japan. Instant decisions are avoided by Japanese personnel. If the fire alarm goes off while we are outside they are down at security finding why it has gone off.

By contrast, however, another respondent replied:

> The parent company has only a relatively small turnover, it's only considered a medium-sized company. This is their first expansion outside the Pacific Rim, so they've given us a lot more leeway than a lot of Japanese companies would.

One of the joint venture respondents replied that 'the parent company's attitude is that if we're doing OK they leave us alone . . . but they like to see us doing *kaizen*'.

The location decision

The location decision rationale has been extensively detailed in all of the previous studies of Japanese investment in Wales. Indeed, for the earlier investments these studies are worth referring back to. In 5 of the firms in our survey, for example, respondents could not answer this question because the personnel involved no longer worked in the company, had transferred elsewhere, etc.

Munday's survey, for example, pointed to nine major factors in the location decision, with the most prominent being labour factors, financial assistance, WDA assistance and infrastructure. The Arthur D. Little survey and the Morris survey both broadly concur with this. These previous findings are broadly replicated in this survey, but there are notable differences, as is indicated in Table 2.10. Twenty firms responded to this question, and the most popularly cited reason for the location decisions was proximity to customers (7). Moreover, this was given as the only location factor in 6 responses. This was hardly mentioned in any of the previous studies and is a reflection that the 'second wave' of Japanese investments in Wales are primarily comprised of supply firms who have located in the first instance to serve the Japanese OEMs in Wales.

Location decision	*No. of times cited*
Proximity to customer	7
Labour availability/cost	6
English language	5
Incentives	4
Take-over	2
Role of WDA	2
Role of local authority	1
Proximity to market	1
Land availability	1

Table 2.10: *Factors in decisions of Japanese companies to locate in Wales*
Source: Authors' Survey, 1992.

The rest of the location decisions mirror more closely the earlier surveys, with labour availability and cost, the use of the English language and the availability of financial incentives all important.

THREE

Japanese Manufacturing Investments in Wales: The Economic Consequences

This chapter will examine both the direct and indirect economic impact of Japanese manufacturing investment upon the Welsh economy. In the first section Japanese investment is set within the context of the economic needs of Wales and the broad objectives of regional policy. The second section of the chapter analyses the direct economic impact of the Japanese investment in terms of job creation and sectoral impact. The third section of the chapter examines the underlying quality of Japanese manufacturing investment in Wales. This includes an examination of the quality of the employment created together with an evaluation of the indirect economic impact of Japanese investment. This section makes extensive use of the survey evidence we gathered during 1992 on Japanese manufacturing investment in Wales. The conclusion of the chapter provides an assessment of the overall economic contribution of this new manufacturing investment, and comments on the extent to which it meets the economic needs of Wales.

Regional policy and the economic needs of Wales

The 1970s and 1980s has witnessed a considerable element of structural change within the Welsh economy. Between 1975 and 1990 the number of employees within production and construction industries fell by 125,000 (nearly 30 per cent), with the most notable changes occurring in metal manufacture/chemicals (a loss of 68,000 jobs) and energy and water supply (a loss of 38,000 jobs). Unemployment in the Welsh economy peaked during 1985 when over 167,000 people were out of work.[1] Between 1975 and 1990 service industry employment grew by 143,000 (27 per cent), and employs around 670,000 people in Wales.

In spite of a period of economic growth during the 1980s, and an excellent record in attracting inward investment, Wales remains behind many other UK regions on a number of key indicators. Welsh GDP per head was 16 per cent lower than the UK average in 1988, and evidence suggests that this gap will increase. The 1980s has also witnessed a growing divide in the Wales/UK earnings ratio. From a position of being relatively high in the pay league during the early 1980s, Wales was at 1992 well towards the bottom. A number of reasons have been put forward for this state of affairs, including a shift of male labour away from the traditionally well-paid manufacturing and mining sectors to the service sector, a shift in employment towards the public sector, and increasing female participation in the Welsh workforce.[2] Simpson suggests that the explanation is found in the changing composition of the workforce, the demise of trade unionism, and the lower level of comparative earnings in the Welsh service sector.[3] Disturbingly, these forces will cause a continued and growing division in the Wales/UK earnings ratio.

Within the Welsh economy itself there are also serious economic disparities in both earnings levels and household income. There are important divides in Wales on leading indicators between the wealthier areas of South-east Wales and Clwyd, and the poorer areas around the South Wales Valleys, West Wales and the rural counties of Dyfed, Powys and Gwynedd.

Hill and Munday concluded that foreign investment within the Welsh economy should be considered within the framework of a need for jobs and incomes in specific areas.[4] Unfortunately, those areas with the greatest needs are often those areas which have the least to offer inwardly investing companies in terms of infrastructure.

Regional policy, as it applies to Wales, has sought to meet the above needs, and to bridge economic divides. One key element of this policy has been the attraction of inward investment from both the wider UK and abroad. The 'pull' policy has taken a variety of formats. Substantial areas of South Wales and Clwyd are classed as intermediate or development areas. Plants locating in these areas are presently allowed a measure of regional selective assistance, which by 1992 has largely superseded the earlier automatic regional development grants. In addition the Welsh Office acts as agent for a number of European Community funds. The Welsh Development Agency (WDA) has built a large quantity of advanced factory space in assisted areas. The international arm of the WDA, Welsh Development International, has also aggressively marketed Wales as a location abroad.

The objectives of the Welsh Office in specifically attracting investment from overseas is clearly set out in its 1988 evidence to the Welsh Affairs Committee:

> The policy of the Welsh Office and the agencies for which it is responsible is to seek to increase the flow [of inward investment] to improve the general prosperity of Wales, and in particular to increase employment opportunities. These benefits come from jobs provided or safeguarded by inward investment projects, through providing additional trading opportunities for industry already located in Wales and through the stimulation of local industry through new ideas.[5]

Hence in summary, the objectives of the policy of attracting foreign investors, are the creation of direct and indirect jobs, together with the creation of a stimulus for new ideas emanating from the presence of multinational capital in the region.

During the 1980s Wales has attracted the highest relative regional proportion of the new foreign owned company projects and jobs coming into the UK (Table 3.1).[6] Between 1979 and 1990 there were 462 reported new foreign projects coming to Wales, with an estimated connected employment of just over 34,000. Recent evidence suggests that during 1991 Wales attracted a further 90 foreign projects, with a total investment of over £700 million, and with the prospect of the creation of over 6,500 jobs within three years. Regional policy has certainly played some part in this continued success. Empirical research suggests that the relative success of the region in attracting foreign investment reflects high relative levels of regional preferential assistance and infrastructure spending, and low relative labour costs in Wales. The importance of relatively low labour costs, and high levels of regional preferential assistance has raised questions about the quality of foreign inward investment coming to Wales.[7] The quality of Japanese manufacturing investment in the region is discussed later in this chapter.

Years	Projects No. of projects	(%UK)	New jobs No. of jobs	(%UK)
1979–81	54	11.5	6,172	12.5
1982–84	90	12.9	6,975	13.1
1985–87	152	14.6	8,834	13.9
1988–90	166	16.0	12,306	14.4

Table 3.1: *New foreign projects and planned new jobs in Wales 1979–90*
Source: Invest in Britain Bureau.

Having set a background of the economic needs of Wales, and the objectives of policy of attracting inward investment, there is now a need to specifically consider the extent to which Japanese manufacturing investment has met the objectives of policy.

New jobs?

Japanese manufacturing companies in Wales have certainly created employment. At the start of the 1980s Japanese firms employed around 2,500 people. By 1985 this figure had risen to 3,500 or 8.2 per cent of total foreign owned production unit employment (1.7 per cent of Welsh manufacturing employment). Between 1985 and 1991 the total employed within Japanese subsidiaries grew very rapidly reaching nearly 12,000 by 1991. Our own employment evidence however indicates that by spring 1992, the 28 Japanese

Sector		*% total*
Consumer electronics/office equipment makers. (SIC 33,34)	8,663	66.5
Components for consumer electronic and office equipment products (SIC var).	1,204	9.2
Vehicle components (SIC 35)	2,118	16.3
Chemicals/process industry (SIC 48)	260	2.0
Other manufacturing (mostly SIC 34)	779	6.0
Total	13,024	100.0

Table 3.2: *Employment in Japanese manufacturing enterprises in Wales by main industrial sector*
Source: Authors' Survey, 1992.

manufacturing enterprises operating in Wales employed over 13,000 people, with a near term forecast of an increase to 17,000 people by the end of 1995.[8] Of this figure of 13,000 jobs, over 85 per cent could be regarded as new as opposed to safeguarded jobs. The breakdown of this Japanese manufacturing employment by broad industrial sector is given in Table 3.2.

Table 3.2 indicates that over 65 per cent of the employment provided has been SIC classes 33 and 34, that is, manufacture of office machinery, data processing equipment, electronic and electrical engineering. The presence of the Japanese manufacturers, and the rapid growth of employment between 1985 and 1992, has added immensely to Welsh employment in this manufacturing sector. The civilian Welsh workforce engaged in employment within SIC 3 grew from 80,000 to 115,000 between 1985 and 1990.

How have new jobs been created?

Data available for the period 1983 to 1991 from the Welsh Office indicate that in comparison to investment coming from European and North American sources, Japanese investment has created proportionately more employment through expansion projects. Table 3.3 shows projects secured and associated employment by international source.

Projects from the Far East (the vast bulk of these are Japanese) accounted for nearly 30 per cent of planned new jobs announced during the period from known foreign sources, and nearly 20 per cent of planned capital investment. Every Japanese project that came to Wales during 1983–91 had, on average, a higher number of connected new jobs associated with it than projects from either North America or Europe. This is because Far Eastern expansion projects during the period had an average planned employment of 154 per project. The Far Eastern average capital expenditure per expansion project is also higher than that for North America and Europe, at £9.43 million per project. Table 3.3 also shows that a high proportion of jobs connected with Japanese projects are new as opposed to safeguarded. This is mainly due to the fact that a high proportion of Japanese companies have set up on greenfield manufacturing sites as opposed to acquiring existing workforces.

To summarize, a substantial proportion of the growth in Japanese company employment through the 1980s has come from

Source	Project type	Number	Planned new jobs	Safeguarded jobs	Planned cap. inv. (£m)
N. America					
	New	77	8,794	1,862	1,021.76
	Exp	113	5,948	9,626	709.35
	Acq/JV	29	212	3,792	92.74
	Total	219	14,954	15,280	1,823.85
Europe					
	New	92	5,965	250	340.35
	Exp	72	3,306	2,792	445.14
	Acq/JV	27	312	3,954	138.23
	Total	191	9,583	6,996	923.73
Japan/Far East					
	New	30	3,135	0	232.21
	Exp	40	6,164	1,390	377.42
	Acq/JV	8	973	25	35.30
	Total	78	10,272	1,415	644.93

Summary Averages. per International source

	North America	*Europe*	*Far East*
Planned new jobs per new project	114	65	105
Planned new jobs per expansion project	53	46	154
Planned new jobs per total projects	68	50	132
Planned cap. exp. per new project (£m)	13.26	3.69	7.74
Planned cap. exp. per expansion project (£m)	6.28	6.18	9.43

Table 3.3: *Foreign inward investment projects secured in the Welsh economy 1983–91*
Source: Welsh Office.
Note: Acq = acquisition; JV = joint venture.

expansions of existing facilities, which is testimony to the rapid growth connected with Japanese plants.

One other important conclusion with respect to Table 3.3 is that the growth of employment from Japanese enterprises (in conjunction with investment from EC firms) has lessened Welsh dependence on the USA and Canada as a source of foreign owned company investment and jobs. In 1974 North American subsidiaries in the Welsh economy accounted for nearly 90 per cent of total foreign owned company manufacturing employment and capital investment.[9] By 1991, the proportion of foreign owned company manufacturing employment attributable to North American firms had dropped to under 50 per cent (33,200 jobs).[10] Between 1980 and 1991, Japanese manufacturing employment has come from a situation of not being separately listed in the statistics, to a situation in 1991 where latest Welsh Office figures estimate that Japanese firms account for nearly 18 per cent of foreign owned company manufacturing employment in Wales. As already indicated this percentage is steadily increasing.

Heavy Welsh dependence on one geographical source of foreign inward investment is clearly undesirable, and this diversification in geographical source aided by Japanese and EC investment together has been a significant recent development.

Cost and location of new jobs

The level of public expenditure associated with the attraction of Japanese or any other foreign investment is very difficult to isolate in total. Financial incentives, subsidized loans, etc., come from a variety of sources. However, it is possible to report the amount of automatic regional development grants (RDGs), and offers of regional selective assistance (RSA) going to individual Japanese firms (see Table 3.4). During the 1980s automatic assistance has gradually been replaced by selective assistance.

Between February 1981 and January 1991 reported regional development grants to 16 Japanese firms in Wales totalled just over £17.5 million. Over 70 per cent of these grants in money terms went to just four Japanese firms, with two large consumer electronic goods manufacturers taking nearly 50 per cent of the total.

Over a similar time period reported offers of regional selective assistance to 16 Japanese enterprises in Wales totalled just over £25 million. Once again a few firms counted for a large amount of this total. The 2 firms that collected 50 per cent of the regional development grants, also collected over 55 per cent of RSA offers, with 4 firms collecting once again over 70 per cent of offers.

Company	RDG	RSA offered
Sony (Bridgend)	3,968	8,100
Sharp (Wrexham)	4,623	6,120
Brother (Wrexham)	1,513	1,113
Yuasa (Ebbw Vale)	2,368	2,100
Star (Tredegar)	932	990
Hitachi (Hirwaun)	442	1,310
Kyushu Mats. (Newport)	—	1,400
Aiwa (Crumlin)	835	560
Matsushita Elec. (Cardiff)	256	1,050
Matsushita Co. (Baglan)	186	1,000
Tsuda (Wrexham)	750	—
Diaplastics (Bridgend)	—	750
Orion (Kenfig)	556	—
Others	1,165	592
Total	17,594	25,085

Table 3.4: *Reported regional development grants and offers of regional selective assistance to Japanese manufacturers in Wales, February 1981–January 1991 (£000)*
Source: British Business, various; *Employment Gazette*, various.

At 1981 Japanese enterprises employed approximately 2,800 people in Wales, and at 1991 the reported figure was around 8,500. On this basis, over the period, RDG per job created/safeguarded was around £3,086, and RSA offers per job created/safeguarded was around £4,400. A very approximate cost per job figure (just on the basis of RDG and RSA offers) is £7,486.

Moving to a consideration of the location of Japanese investment, Hill and Munday,[11] examining the scope of foreign direct investment in Wales, suggested that in overall terms the location decisions of recent inward investors had done little to aid the economic conditions of areas of Wales hardest hit by structural realignments at the start of the 1980s. Table 3.5 shows the location of employment in Japanese enterprise as at spring 1992.

Around 60 per cent of the employment created by Japanese manufacturing investment is clustered around Newport, Wrexham, Cardiff and Bridgend. In South Wales, at least, the placement of new Japanese enterprise would seem to be reinforcing existing spatial divides in the Welsh economy, with much of the investment

	No. of firms	Employment
Clwyd	8	2,151
Wrexham area	7	1,997
Other	1	154
Dyfed	1	828
Gwent	6	2,025
Newport area	3	1,099
Valley Heads	2	900
Other	1	26
Mid-Glam	7	3,951
Bridgend	3	2,695
Merthyr/Hirwaun	2	930
Other	2	326
West Glam	3	1,879
South Glam	3	2,190

Table 3.5: *Japanese manufacturing company employment by location*
Source: Authors' Survey, 1992.

clustered on what is essentially the M4 corridor. Such a placement pattern is to some extent inevitable given the infrastructure and labour requirements of such firms. It is also noted that some of the larger firms draw workforces from the larger geographical area surrounding plants. In the case of Japanese manufacturers in Cardiff and Bridgend the labour catchment area includes some of the South Wales valleys hit hardest by structural readjustment during the 1970s and 1980s.

The quality of Japanese inward investment

Whilst jobs created and sustained is one measure of regional economic impact it is also important to analyse the underlying quality of Japanese manufacturing investment in Wales. In part this entails an examination of the nature of employment created. However, there are also other questions that must be addressed concerning the indirect economic impact of such investments. Wales has been described as a classic branch plant economy where incoming manufacturing plants generally are characterized by:

a. a limited scale of research and development;
b. limited plant-level autonomy and few higher-level management functions;
c. few local purchasing linkages;
d. few instances of local technical linkages and industrial cooperation.

Where plants are characterized by these factors the regional economic regenerative potential may be seriously affected.[12]

Thus in examining the quality of Japanese manufacturing investment there is also a need to analyse the extent to which these characteristics are in place. Only then is it possible to comment on present, and more importantly future economic impact.

The nature of the new employment

The quality of employment created by Japanese manufacturing investments has been a regular topic of political and economic debate in Wales. Such concerns are relevant because there is the fear that inwardly investing firms come to peripheral locations just to take advantage of low factor costs, while gaining access to core markets. The main areas of concern with respect to the quality of employment are as follows:

a. that the incoming manufacturing plants provide a high quantity of employment for females and school leavers (i.e. low cost labour);
b. that the jobs provided are of an unskilled and very routine nature, which reduces the job experience of employees, and the economic regenerative potential of inward investments;
c. that there are few opportunities of employment within Japanese plants for those who have been made unemployed in more traditional industrial segments.

Females make up just over 50 per cent of the Japanese company workforce in Wales: in all the cases where there was a higher proportion of female participation, plant operations could be described as high volume assembly/manufacture. All the major producers of consumer electronic goods and office machinery had

Female as % workforce	*Number of enterprises*
0–19	7
20–39	2
40–49	3
50–59	3
60–69	4
70–79	5
Over 80	1

Table 3.6: *Female participation in Japanese companies in Wales (N = 25)*
Source: Authors' Survey, 1992.

female labour forces making up 50–70 per cent of the total. Such a high proportion is expected given that many of the Japanese manufacturers in this sector require dextrous skills in electronic goods assembly. Female employment as a percentage of total Japanese subsidiary workforces in Wales would seem to be decreasing over time as automation removes many assembly tasks, and as some components production has been brought in house by major manufacturers. For details of female participation see Table 3.6.

Lower levels of female participation (less than 40 per cent of the total) are to be found in Japanese companies which could not be described as assemblers. This included three companies in the broad chemicals sector and four components makers. Only two of the nine firms having lower numbers of female workers employed over 500 people.

At 1992 few Japanese manufacturers reported that their workforces were made up of a high proportion of school leavers. Six companies reported that they had begun operations in Wales by taking on a high proportion of school leavers, but had since tried to develop workforces characterized by greater age ranges, to promote stability. This had occurred because firms had suffered problems of high turnover, indiscipline and absence. Hence, in 1992, Japanese company workforces in Wales are characterized by a greater range of ages than has previously been the case, with some new firms being 'scared off' from using school leavers by the problems of established firms. In three of the larger consumer electronics companies in South Wales, which in total employed nearly

5,000 people, the average age of workforce was around 27. Evidence would thus tend to suggest that school leavers and younger employees are becoming a smaller proportion of Japanese company workforces in Wales, and that there are thus increasing opportunities for those more mature workers who have been displaced by structural change in established Welsh industrial segments.

The jobs provided by the Japanese subsidiaries cover a number of levels from unskilled through to professional. The majority of jobs provided could be described as being of a semi-skilled nature. There are opportunities within the larger factories to rotate jobs, and to learn other tasks on the line. Multi-tasking is a precursor to further shopfloor promotion in many factories, and is also a factor favourably looked upon within internal appraisal. In these cases the job experience of factory personnel is widened to a limited degree. With the continued automation of routine assembly tasks many of the most boring jobs will continue to be reduced in the future. A large element of the routine will, however, survive in many of the larger Japanese factories. To counter the routine, some local Japanese firms create fresh challenges by continued development of their local workforces. This is evidenced by a strong in-house training emphasis that is noted later on in this volume.

Local purchasing linkages

A key objective of policy in bringing foreign investment to Wales was the creation of trading opportunities for local firms. In this context 'local' is taken to mean within the confines of the regional economy. Definitions of local are important here for to many inward foreign investors local content may mean EC content. The existence of trading opportunities is important to the local economy. Payments by Japanese companies into the Welsh economy do not just go to suppliers. Considerable amounts of money are involved in the preparation of industrial sites and infrastructure, the construction of factories for Japanese firms and to support services more generally. Payments made in the Welsh economy to both suppliers and service industries will have additional multiplier effects reinforcing the indirect employment created or sustained by the payments. The potential effects are schematically summarised in Figure 3.1.

In addition to these possible trading opportunities for local suppliers, linkages with Japanese investors may provide the basis

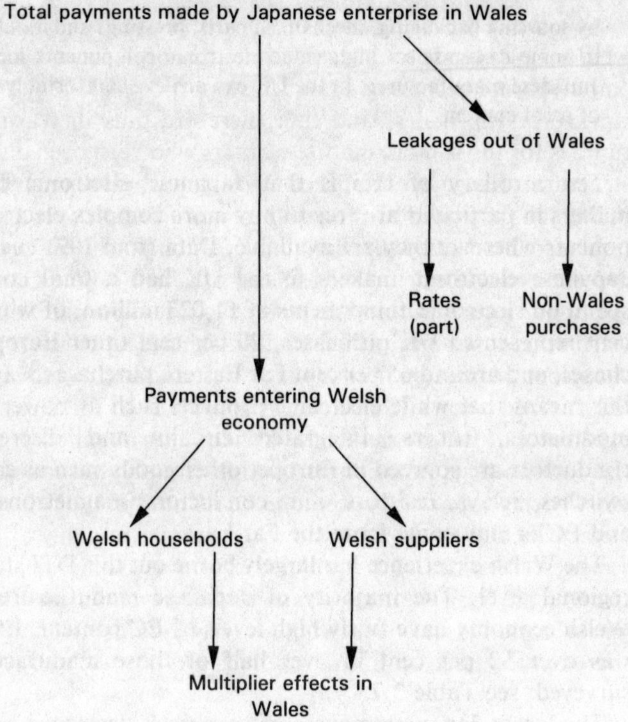

Figure 3.1 Total payments made by Japanese enterprise in Wales

for the transfer of new ideas and 'best practice' in operational technique.

Precise detail on the extent of local trading linkages and multiplier effects is difficult to assess because firms will rarely divulge the level of local spending. However, it is possible to comment on the nature of Japanese trading linkages in the local economy, and the extent of diffusion of best practice to locally based suppliers.

Japanese firms manufacturing in Wales do not have to purchase in Wales to meet either present or perceived future pressures on local content levels. In fact, by purchasing only certain types of selected components within the EC Japanese firms are normally able to meet EC requirements on local content levels. According to a Department of Trade and Industry sponsored report on the demand being created for electronic components by Japanese electrical equipment makers in the UK:

> by sourcing packaging, mechanical parts, pressings and mouldings, and in some cases, select high value electronic components locally, most Japanese manufacturers in the UK can achieve comfortably high levels of local content.[13]

The corollary of this is that Japanese electronic equipment makers in particular are free to buy more complex electronic components wherever they are available. Data from 1991 suggests that Japanese electronic makers in the UK had a total components spend on electronic components of £1,023 million, of which 15 per cent represented UK purchases, 20 per cent other European purchases, and around 65 per cent Far Eastern purchases.[14] In practice this means that while electronic products such as power supplies, modulators, tuners, integrated circuits and discrete semi-conductors are sourced in Europe, other goods such as capacitors, switches, relays, resistors, semi-conductors, magnetrons, crystals and PCBs may come from the Far East.

The Welsh experience has largely borne out this DTI study at the regional level. The majority of Japanese manufacturers in the Welsh economy have fairly high levels of EC content. EC content was over 50 per cent in over half of those manufacturers we surveyed: see Table 3.7.

The larger Japanese makers of consumer electronics equipment all had local content in excess of 50 per cent, with the common range being 60–80 per cent variable by product. Highest levels of local content were found in those firms within the plastic processing/chemicals sector. Three of these firms actually had local

Content level (%)	*Number of enterprises*
0–20	5
21–40	1
41–60	2
61–80	2
81–100	8
Not specified	6

Table 3.7: *EC content levels in the main products of Japanese enterprises in Wales at April 1992. (N = 24).*
Source: Authors' Survey, 1992.

content in excess of 95 per cent. Lower levels of EC content were normally found in recently established Japanese enterprises producing either electronic components or sub-assemblies for the consumers electronics and office automation goods sectors.

Whilst Japanese firms reported that a high proportion of products came from Europe, many smaller electronic components are still purchased in the Far East. One electronic equipment manufacturer reported that whilst 70 per cent of its parts *by value* came from Europe, 85 per cent of parts by *number* came from the Far East. The Far East remains an important source for smaller components because:

a. purchasing economies are available where the parent company in Japan buys for its worldwide network of subsidiaries;
b. where purchasing links in the Far East are already in place, the search costs in redirecting the business for a multitude of small parts would be greater than any marginal benefit;
c. where products have been designed in Japan, then components are often designed around the product, meaning that EC sources of such components are simply unavailable.

The purchase of components in Wales is fairly limited. The most commonly bought Welsh made components include products such as plastic components and mouldings, metal pressings, metal parts, cartons and packaging, printed materials, and a limited number of more complex components which were often being produced by Japanese suppliers who have come to Wales.

Whilst the amount that most Japanese enterprises buy in the Welsh economy is necessarily limited, they have at the same time been keen to buy as much locally as possible. Sony at Bridgend is a good example:

> It is the policy of Sony to place as much business with Welsh suppliers as possible. To this end, we are actively developing existing supply sources, encouraging new suppliers to come into areas where there are gaps in the supply base, and via the Welsh Quality Centre, we are actively involved in promoting quality as the most important issue.[15]

It has been in the interests of some Japanese assemblers to purchase as much as possible within a close radius of plant site. Pressures in both physical and cost terms upon factory space have ensured the use of systems emphasizing the accelerated flow of material through plants, prompt delivery of components, and limited inventory holdings. In such a productive environment concise management of the supply chain is a must, not least when supplies are heavy and bulky. In these special circumstances geographical proximity of suppliers aids the management process. Thus some Japanese companies in Wales have actively worked to develop the local supply infrastructure as far as is possible. This development has both sustained and created some indirect employment. For example, if one examines suppliers of plastic-injected moulded components, a bulky component that Japanese manufacturers have been keen to buy within Wales, then indirect employment has come through a number of routes:

a. Where existing indigenous suppliers have attracted Japanese business.
b. Where locally based suppliers have diversified to meet Japanese demands. For example. Otford Group had been supplying Japanese manufacturers in Wales with expanded polystyrene packaging for many years. However, in response to local Japanese demands for high-quality plastic moulded components the company firm set up a specialized mouldings division during 1987.
c. Where existing suppliers to Japanese enterprise enter the region to support Japanese demands, i.e. for geographical proximity and delivery. This may mean existing suppliers from the UK, EC or Japan. For example Caradon Elliot (Walsall), Nincaplast (Germany), and Tsuda and Diaplastics from Japan, have all come to Wales to support Japanese demands for plastic mouldings.

Other supply subsets in metal pressings, electronic sub-assembly, printing, electronic harnesses, etc., have followed similar patterns. Precise estimation of indirect employment creation through Japanese demands is not a straightforward calculation, but it is estimated that the plastic injection moulding supplier subset alone employs over 500 people, of which a high percentage is due to Japanese demand.

Local trading linkages with Japanese manufacturers do have a further economic significance. Such linkages are also a possible means of transferring 'best practice' operational techniques. The Japanese have been keen to develop with their Welsh-based suppliers partnership-based relationships, as opposed to the more traditional style of buyer–supplier relationship where links are short term, with an emphasis on quoted price and little shared information. Closer buyer–supplier relationships revolve around mutual commitment over the longer term, with information as well as the risks and rewards of the partnership being shared. In practical terms the Japanese orientation towards closer buyer–supplier relationships indicates a recognition that coordination and cooperation with suppliers is a necessity if waste and inefficiency are to be removed within the supply chain. In practical terms the 'partnership principle' tends to link the manufacturer on a long term basis, with a smaller number of carefully selected suppliers, where information on components production and final usage is shared to aid technical collaboration and development work.

During 1990 a section of suppliers to Japanese industry in Wales were surveyed by Munday[16] to find evidence of the existence of this 'partnership principle' and of collaborative relationships between buyer and supplier. During 1992, the present authors' survey of Japanese manufacturers in Wales also sought to find evidence on the nature of buyer–supplier partnerships. A number of common themes came to the fore in these studies. Japanese manufacturers had been extremely careful in selecting their Welsh suppliers. Suppliers were rarely selected on the basis of price alone. In some instances buyers had carefully audited supplier facilities. Such audits examined manufacturing procedures, order processing, back up systems, scheduling, calibration of equipment, general housekeeping, and management attitudes. Although it had often taken some time to win Japanese business, once established, linkages were sustained over the long term. Winning business with one Japanese manufacturer was often a precursor to winning contracts with other Japanese plants in both Wales and the wider UK, and several Welsh suppliers noted that once the linkage was in place volumes had grown very quickly. In some circumstances such suppliers had no longer needed to advertise but had just to manage growth and quality. Buyer–supplier linkages were characterized by regular communication. Suppliers perceived a genuine desire amongst Japanese plants to aid them in problem solving.

Surveyed suppliers in Wales noted a number of benefits as a result of their linkage with Japanese enterprise. The partnership principle tends to push a greater level of responsibility on to the supplier. Suppliers noted that more attention was given to detail with respect to operational processes. As part of communication the provision of cost information from supplier to buyer aided value analysis. Suppliers had been obliged to take on board Japanese quality standards throughout their processes and this had aided them in winning other business. The long-run nature of the purchasing linkages had given some suppliers the stability to undertake longer-term investment decision making, and production and resource planning. Also, suppliers noted that whilst Japanese clients required prompt delivery of components, they were likewise extremely prompt in paying accounts.

Where partnerships had developed the Japanese were often anxious to extend the nature of linkage. In some circumstances component makers had become involved in additional sub-assembly work connected with their products. Only in a few circumstances had suppliers taken on responsibility for design and development of components. Suppliers were usually happy with these developments because it consolidated their long term linkage with the Japanese.

Whilst the above factors are generally very positive, both surveys picked up some potential problems. Suppliers had often found it difficult to pass on price increases, as Japanese firms expected prices to fall as volumes pushed to suppliers increased. The requirements of supplier auditing programmes of buyers were sometimes seen as an intrusion, especially where such audits required details of cost breakdowns of components.[17] Finally, the Japanese requirement for just-in-time delivery sometimes left suppliers with high levels of buffer stocks. However, in spite of some problems the general tone of local supply linkages with Japanese subsidiaries was positive and growing.

In conclusion, whilst Japanese purchasing links in the Welsh economy have been somewhat limited, there is evidence of the creation of local indirect employment. In addition, local suppliers who have won contracts have benefited from their close linkages with the Japanese in operational and commercial terms. Some elements of best practice have certainly been transferred into local firms.

Plant level autonomy and scale of R&D

Gauging the level of autonomy within local Japanese plants is a complex problem. There is no single indicator of the level of autonomy of a manufacturing plant from its corporate headquarters. Yet, the level of plant autonomy is always an important consideration. A foreign plant that is run tightly by its corporate headquarters many thousands of miles away may not always be operated with the full local economic context in view. There is often the spectre of decisions having a crucial bearing on the future of the Welsh economy being taken with little consideration of the local impact.

Japanese plants in the Welsh economy are large enough to create significant local economic effects, as well as both social and environmental externalities. It is important that any resultant effects emanating from the presence of Japanese manufacturing subsidiaries harmonize with local social and economic policy. Where locally based management has either little decision-making capacity or is not committed to the needs of the host region, any positive impact potential may be reduced.

As previously stated, there is no single indicator of local plant level autonomy. It is possible, however, to get an indication of autonomy from an examination of the strength of communications linkages with corporate head offices, and the extent of corporate monitoring of subsidiary activities.

In our survey, 20 Japanese manufacturers gave details of reporting links. In 14 cases these reporting linkages were straight back to Japanese head offices rather than to European offices. In 3 other cases the reporting linkage was complex due to joint venture agreements. With only 3 Japanese enterprises was the initial reporting linkage to a European office. Very few Japanese parent companies have gone far towards localizing reporting structures. There are some notable exceptions to this. Since 1989 Panasonic has regionalized its European operations under Panasonic (Europe). This head office covers the whole operating scenario from research and development, production, distribution, customer support and personnel. However, the strong divisional structure of the Matsushita organization still ensures close reporting links to Japan. Sony have also tried to move to localization of its European activities. Most of its European operations are well integrated, and have been supplemented by European based R&D activity.

In the majority of cases communication with Japanese head office or parent is on a daily basis. The telephone bills in a number of plants are reported as being colossal. Fax and telephone communication with Japan is dominated by Japanese expatriate staff. The content of daily communications was varied but in the sixteen enterprises giving details the following was typical:

a. Communication on technical matters and problem solving. This communication for example might include information relating to the use of local components and design.
b. Ordering of components and kits from the Far East, or in some cases communication to aid the transferral of business from Japanese to local plants.
c. Sales and marketing information on both products and components.
d. Personal matters involving Japanese staff.

Two local managers, one in a large consumer electronics subsidiary, and one in a smaller components firm, summed up the daily communication patterns in the following terms:

> Communication is very frequent. Faxes come to and fro for most of the day . . . a wide variety . . . they are not always faxes that require a decision but may be faxes providing information. The Japanese tend to stay late at night to exchange faxes with Japan.

And:

> Our fax machine is a hot machine. This is because head office makes many decisions . . . our telephone bill is horrific . . . this communication is nearly all done by Japanese managers here. Only one person in the Japanese company can speak English.

Actual plant performance monitoring by Japanese head offices was usually carried out on a monthly basis, although in one plant in North Wales monitoring was on a weekly basis. The main monitoring linkage was via a monthly report which as well as giving details of financial ratios, profit and loss, budget variance and output, would also in some instances provide details on productivity, development work, reject rates, local component usage, and a number of quality parameters.

Typically, within the Japanese plants surveyed there was a measure of autonomy is some areas. One manager in a Japanese maker of electronic components described the situation in the following terms:

> There is a lot of communication with Japan but business plans are made here. However, these have to be agreed with Japan. At the moment our people are in Japan getting the business plan authorised. Investment is based on what we can afford . . . if we want more we have to go to Japan. Our capital base is low, so if we borrow we need their security. New product decision making would also be done in Japan. Although much work is done here we often rely on information from other sections. On the personnel side there is more autonomy from the Japanese headquarters.

This type of experience seemed common. Although there is some autonomy with respect to the day-to-day running of plants, major strategic decision making is done in conjunction with Japan. The absolute level of autonomy does vary from firm to firm. In some limited instances there was evidence of tight control from head offices even on day to day matters.

The evidence on communication linkage and plant monitoring points to a set of Japanese subsidiaries in Wales with strong links to head office. This is further evidenced by the position of Japanese personnel within subsidiaries. There are a number of sound reasons for the presence of Japanese personnel at the local level. Expatriate management aid the communication process. Japanese engineers are often needed to aid the transfer of technology and processes from the Japanese parent organization, and to manage change.[18] Within the majority of Japanese plants the number of Japanese expatriates is quickly reducing. Although it is expensive for the parent to retain expatriate personnel in Wales, Japanese personnel still retain a number of key positions in plant hierarchies. Our survey indicated that in the 25 Japanese enterprises giving details that there were just over 200 Japanese staff. In only 6 cases were there more than 10 Japanese in a plant. In 15 cases there were 5 or fewer. Larger concentrations of Japanese staff are found in the producers of consumer electronics goods. Within the 29 Japanese manufacturing enterprises in Wales all but 7 still have a Japanese expatriate manager at the helm. Other Japanese personnel appear in a variety of roles, usually in technical, developmental, financial and quality management functions. In some cases Japanese managers sit as advisers to local senior management, and there is some evidence that policies of shadowing local employees with Japanese personnel has caused resentment.[19] Japanese personnel have thus been retained in many key positions within subsidiary organizational structures.

In summary, the evidence on plant monitoring, reporting linkages and placement of expatriate personnel indicates that the Japanese plants in Wales generally have low levels of autonomy and decision making authority. This finding would appear to be at variance with the conclusions of the Japanese External Trade Organization (1992) report on Japanese investment in Europe on this matter.[20] JETRO felt that there had been substantial devolution of decision-making powers to the European affiliates over a range of functions from personnel to R&D. For most of the Japanese subsidiaries in Wales at least, decision-making authority on a number of strategic issues would appear to rest in Japan.

In the light of the above discussion it is perhaps not surprising that the scale of research and development carried out by Japanese plants in Wales is still somewhat limited. The presence of extensive research and development functions within subsidiaries can add greatly to the quality of the subsidiary involvement. R&D requires substantial investment in facilities and people, and importantly the presence of such functions can lead to significant technically based spin-offs in the local economy. The absence of R&D is often reflected in a plant's dependence upon the parent for new technology and products. Young[21] suggests that surveys of inward investment generally in Wales show little in the way of larger-scale fundamental research and development, with the position least encouraging amongst the Japanese.

Our own survey found that 9 out of 23 Japanese enterprises said that they were actually participating in R&D. However, it was clear from the survey that the majority of the plants were involved in some type of development or design work. As manufacturing operations have been gradually localized by Japanese parent companies then design and development work is needed to modify Japanese designed models for local usage. Furthermore, a great deal of development work is involved to both test and adapt locally produced components, and to design tooling, etc. Thus whilst there are few instances of pure research activities in the Japanese subsidiaries there is considerable evidence of both design and development work. Sony, for example, has 50 to 60 development engineers at Bridgend involved with colour television developments. Calsonic at Llanelli has around 80 people employed within its R&D function, which does research on materials and processes, as well as product development.

The absence of more basic research functions is also evidenced by the small number of graduates employed by Japanese firms in Wales. Our study suggested that in 22 enterprises which provided details of UK graduate employment (or equivalent), 16 had 10 graduates or under, a further 5 had between 11 and 25 graduates, with just 1 company (Sony) having over 100 graduates (the 22 enterprises providing this information excluded one other Japanese company which may have a significant number of graduates). The absence of more basic research may go some way towards explaining the generally low level of technical collaboration/industrial cooperation between local Japanese subsidiaries and local organizations in the region (excluding suppliers) which was evidenced. The links established by Japanese firms in their local communities are more fully dealt with in Chapter 7.

It is noted that several Japanese firms with plants in Wales do have European-based centres for advanced research work into new products. For example, Panasonic has R&D facilities in Germany which are working around new generation CTV systems. Hitachi has a research centre at Cambridge, and Sharp Laboratories is moving into new facilities on the Oxford Science Park.

Conclusions

In this chapter an attempt has been made to evaluate the economic consequences of Japanese manufacturing investment upon the Welsh economy. There is little doubt that the overall economic contribution from the Japanese subsidiaries has been positive. Employment creation during the 1980s has been substantial, and is set to grow even further as Japanese operations in Wales expand further when the UK/European market comes out of recession. The employment created has also added to industry sector diversity in the Welsh economy, and has also lessened Welsh dependence on North America as a source of foreign company employment. Whilst the direct economic impact in terms of jobs created is substantial, questions of indirect economic impact remain more problematical.

The nature of employment created has been a topic of some debate. Local Japanese subsidiaries have been criticized for using high numbers of school leavers and female staff in low skill tasks. Thus whilst the employment created was great, the quality of employment was low. Whilst such conclusions are true with respect to a limited number of Japanese enterprises in Wales, they are not wholly true in the case of the majority. Our study found evidence of a decreasing proportion of female/school leaver participation in some Japanese subsidiary workforces. There was also evidence in some subsidiaries of a commitment to actively train and develop the local workforce.

The local purchasing linkages of Japanese enterprises in Wales remain limited for what are often sound economic reasons. However, once again there is evidence of growing local purchasing linkages. This has led in some cases to the development of local subcontracting complexes in products such as metal pressings, and plastic injection mouldings. The purchasing linkages that do exist have also been a mechanism for the transfer of operational best practice in a number of instances. However, payments going into the Welsh economy via local purchases have been limited, as will be any resultant multiplier effects from this source.

The Japanese plants remain fairly closely linked to their parent companies in Japan, and evidence suggests that plant-level autonomy is limited in the majority of cases. This is also reflected in low levels of research and development among the plants. Whilst the Japanese subsidiaries carry out product development work, pure research is comparatively rare. Subsidiaries are normally dependent on their parent companies for both new products and technology. It is suggested that this will limit any potential technical spin-offs resulting from the presence of the investments.

In overall terms then, the economic effects are mixed. Whilst there has been a substantial direct employment effect, question marks about the underlying quality of the Japanese investments still persist. What is clear, however, is that these questions of underlying quality also apply to other inward investments not just the Japanese. In part the presence of the Japanese has gone some way to meeting the objectives of regional policy and the economic needs of Wales.

FOUR
Work, Organization and Management

The Japanese form of production organization is in many ways different to the forms experienced by most British workers, requiring employees, for instance, to work in teams, to accept to undertake different tasks, to accept responsibility for the quality of their work, and to subject themselves to strict discipline. Such an experience of work derives in large part from the use of just-in-time (JIT) production and total quality controls (TQC).[1] Just-in-time, as the name suggests, is a form of production characterized by producing what is required exactly when it is required. Within the factory this means that buffer stocks and work-in-progress are kept to a minimum; workers are typically organized into teams, and each team produces according to the demands of its downstream customer team, sometimes indicated on *kanban* cards.[2]

Total quality control, on the other hand, represents an attempt to make quality (defined as the satisfaction of customer needs) the responsibility of everyone, rather than simply that of specialist quality staff. Close monitoring and frequent feedback on quality performance means that faults or mistakes are quickly pinpointed to teams or individuals, who in principle are responsible for making amends. A JIT/TQC system is characterized generally by a delegation of responsibility, and accountability, to the level of the team, which means teams take on some of the tasks which traditionally would be undertaken by specialist groups; as well as quality control, the team must have the capability to undertake routine maintenance, housekeeping, machine setting and production scheduling.[3]

Overarching what Nissan's personnel director, Peter Wickens, has called a Japanese 'tripod' of working practices – quality consciousness, teamwork and flexibility[4] – is the obsession with *kaizen* or 'continuous improvement', a value which, according to one author, derives from Japanese Buddhism.[5] *Kaizen* is associated most obviously with the desire to produce with zero defects and never to be satisfied with quality performance, no matter how close one is to 100 per cent. It also applies to waste elimination, including both material (scrap, machine downtime, stocks) and human waste. Human waste is attacked by continuously trying to improve labour productivity through flexible labour deployment, careful industrial engineering, and the constant measurement of performance against targets. Waste is anything which adds cost but not value to a product, and includes any labour 'idle time' which has been paid for.[6]

The first question we must answer is to what extent Japanese manufacturers in Wales have introduced Japanese forms of production organization within their factories. During our 1992 study we were able to answer this question in detail through interviews with production and operations staff, and through observations of working practices on shopfloors. In all of the companies visited, managers were well versed in Japanese production methods, and there had been a significant, and in many respects successful, attempt to transplant JIT and TQC on to Welsh soil. Table 4.1 shows the number of companies which had adopted, at least partially, specific Japanese forms of production organization.

The remainder of this chapter will describe the realities of production organization and working practices characteristic of the

Just-in-time production	15
Kanban material controls	5
Statistical process control	12
Quality circles	11
Kaizen teams	5
Team-based organization	18
Individual fault tracing	14

Table 4.1: *Usage of Japanese forms of production organization in Japanese companies in Wales (N = 22)*
Source: Authors' Survey, 1992.

Japanese manufacturing transplants we have studied. In so doing we hope to provide the readers with a picture of 'what it is like' to work for a Japanese manufacturer in Wales. For the sake of convenience we have divided the chapter into discussions of production control, quality control, teamwork and discipline, and finally, the roles of team leaders and managers in the shopfloor hierarchy.

Production control and continuous improvement

Of the 22 companies from which we gained an understanding of production organization 15 used JIT, although sometimes on a limited basis between certain processes, and only 5 used *kanban* material flow controls. However, in almost all cases work-in-progress (WIP) and stocks were strictly monitored and controlled, typically goods were 'pulled' through the factory on the basis of production schedules derived from final customer demand, and teams of workers within the factory were encouraged to conceive of downstream workers as their customers. Any limitations on full-blown JIT production were typically related to supply of materials and demand for finished goods (see Chapter 3) rather than to shortcomings in production control within the factory.

Within most factories, there would be negligible or no stocks within processes, and stocks ranging from an hour's to two days' worth between processes, e.g. sub-assembly and final assembly. In one company a highly automated production system uses electronic proximity sensors; goods are pulled through the system at the speed at which they are removed following the final process. Any problem means the whole system grinds to a halt very quickly because there are neither buffers nor the space for buffers to rely on.

In most cases production lines were dedicated to product families – for instance, there would be separate lines for CTVs of different sizes – but were at the same time flexible, so that lines could easily be rejigged to fit in with any changing patterns of demand. In one case the latter was achieved via mobile work stations: individual stations could easily be moved, and production lines reconfigured in a variety of ways to suit changes in model design or demand.

Shopfloor workers were, in most cases, organized into teams of around 15 to 30 members, each team having a clearly defined responsibility for meeting production and quality targets, with their performance being closely monitored and constantly improved upon. The extent to which responsibilities were devolved to teams varied significantly between companies – at the extreme one joint-venture company was introducing a system whereby each team would have control over a budget and be self-managing, to the extent that team leaders would not be appointed but elected. In 5 companies operators were trained in the maintenance of their own machinery and equipment, and in 9 they were trained in statistical process control (SPC). In virtually all cases teams were held accountable for output, quality, materials handling, and above all meeting the demands of their customer. This contrasts with the traditional British situation, where specialists take responsibility for many such activities. Some specialists, especially quality controllers, still exist in the Japanese transplants, but as far as practicable each team has its own capability, and those specialists located in, say, a quality department, are answerable to the team. Departmental empire building is actively discouraged.

Whilst the day to day allocation of tasks within the team was in most cases a responsibility of the team leader (see below), the level of staffing for each team was determined by industrial engineers on the basis of precise calculations of labour requirements against production schedule and standard times. The latter were normally derived from the Japanese parent company, with allowances added on for local circumstances, such as anticipated absences, learning curves on new models, and any differences in equipment and machinery. Teams of workers are then expected to achieve or exceed targets, with output being recorded on an hourly, and sometimes real-time, basis.

In many cases target, actual, cumulative and variance figures are displayed. Negative variances are a serious cause for concern, demanding speedy investigation and corrective action. Positive variances could also be subject to investigation: the indication could be over-staffing, and ultimately new standards and tougher targets could be set, any detailed improvements being diffused through the organization. Industrial engineers, having set up and 'balanced' a line to make a new product or component – a large part of which involves determining an optimum division of labour – then look for detailed improvements. In one case this meant that every job on every line was timed twice a day in the search for improvements in *takt* times (work-cycle times). One manager explained that

> the girls get really bored if they're not busy. They don't like the line stopping and they like a fast *takt* time so they can go smoothly without getting bored. They can switch off while they're working.

At one company detailed improvements were sought through the targetting of bottlenecks – the lowest common denominator which determines the speed of the production line. After a bottleneck – usually a person, but occasionally a machine or robot – had been 'identified, targeted and cured', then either the line speed (and production targets) would be increased, or an individual would be taken out of the team and the line rebalanced (i.e. that individual's tasks would be shared among other team members). The engineers can then seek out the next bottleneck in a never-ending process of continuous improvement. This is one sense in which *kaizen* is built into the system of production.[7]

At another company a model-line which was deliberately staffed by the best supervisors, technicians, and other support, was used to demonstrate 'best practice'. Team leaders, technicians, etc., from other lines were encouraged to observe 'model line' activities and to implement 'best practices' on their own lines. The same company reports on performance to Japan every night, and there are occasional meetings between staff of sister plants in Singapore, Japan, Malaysia and Wales to share ideas and transfer improvements. Performance comparisons and detailed improvements are communicated and discussed right down to operator level.

With very tight staffing policies (slack labour is 'waste') team leaders are faced at the start of every shift with the problem of allocating tasks amongst employees. An allowance for absence is typically built in, but if, say, 3 out of a team of 30 are absent, this could constitute a mini-crisis. In this situation team leaders are often allowed to 'cross-trade' team members in negotiations with other team leaders, and/or to make fine adjustments to the balance of the line (share the absentee's tasks among other members). Certainly, team leaders are usually hard pressed to achieve production targets, and in the absence of slack labour have a real interest in controlling absence and lateness among team members.[8]

Another means of coping with absence or lateness is for the 'float', or even the team leader her/himself, to take a place on the production line. As well as filling in for late-comers, staff visiting the toilet, etc., floats have many other tasks, such as delivering materials to the line and administering quality systems. Typically, there will be around 1 float per 10 employees. One company's continuous improvement programme included reducing the number of floats per employee across the organization from 1 in 7 to 1 in 16. This would put even more pressure on the team leader to ensure lateness and absenteeism were kept to a minimum.

Drives and campaigns to improve efficiency, reduce waste, and improve quality, are commonplace, often with specific targets set for teams or departments. Achievements against targets are displayed on factory walls or communicated through briefings and company newsletters. The *kaizen* philosophy is not something any organizational member could easily ignore.

Hence, although in only 5 cases did we document formal *kaizen* teams, continuous improvement was typically built in to the organization of production through industrial engineering, constant performance measurement and feedback, and the use of devices such as bottleneck targeting and model lines.

Quality control

Perhaps even more than 'customers' and 'continuous improvement', 'quality' was an integral part of managers' vocabulary. It is difficult to walk more than a few yards in a Japanese factory in Wales without seeing the word 'quality' in large bold letters as part of a slogan.

In around half of the cases in our study, quality circles were used. In one company every single employee was a member of a quality circle which would meet in company time at least once a month. In another company with around 80 active quality circles, the circle winning an annual competition would be awarded £250 plus a trip to Japan to make a presentation at a QC convention for all the company's organizations across the world. Managers in this company, like other companies, stressed the importance of staff training and development and the generation of workforce motivation which was necessary before a voluntary quality circle movement could become successful. The more recently arrived manufacturers were less likely to have widespread quality circles, their managers sometimes expressing the opinion that more basic developments are necessary first. For instance, a company which had acquired a British-owned plant in South Wales in 1989 had so far made incremental improvements to the production process, introduced internal education for operators on basic production and quality-control techniques, established a suggestion scheme, and given operators responsibility for routine machine maintenance (a 'my-machine' system). A manager explained that the company had

> done significant work in preparing workers for change . . . We made many incremental improvements to the production process through our continuous improvement programme. In Japan we have very active small quality groups. We intend to introduce them here, but first we're making basic changes, and training and educating workers.

Perhaps more fundamental to quality control than quality circles is making operators and teams responsible and accountable for the quality of their work under a 'right first time' philosophy, and the ability of management to identify and pinpoint any faults, trace them back to point of occurrence, and take the measures necessary to prevent the mistake happening again. Such a philosophy and capability was in evidence on all the shopfloors we visited. Typically, teams are held accountable for any shortfalls regarding levels of scrap or rejects, or indeed for causing any problems for their downstream customers. One company had established formal quality contracts between customer and supplier teams, and members of these teams were expected to meet briefly twice a day to discuss customer satisfaction, any problems, and what might be done to make improvements. Similarly, in another company work teams were briefed by their leader at the start of every shift by a 'customer satisfaction scoreboard' which displayed quality, target, output and other data. Teams were generally responsible for monitoring, documenting and displaying their own quality performance, often through a member frequently visiting the customer team to gather information and feed it back.

Team leaders are often aided in their ability to identify and rectify problems through individual fault-tracing mechanisms. These are based on inspections and tests, which might be visual or electronic, at many stages in the production process. Within each team operators are expected to note any defects or faults caused by their upstream colleagues, and some are dedicated to checking the integrity of the product. Any defects which are passed on to the customer team are likely to be discovered here and made public, adding to the imperative for teams not to pass on faulty product. Inspections and tests are, as far as possible, capable of indicating the precise nature of any fault, so that it can be traced back, not only to the team, but to the individual employee responsible, and because production is just-in-time, or at least with minimum buffer stocks, feedback of the problem to the individual is speedy. One company actually worked on a principle of short feedback loops: operators making mistakes (or those responsible for machines causing faults) would be made aware of the problem within a matter of hours at most, and sometimes within minutes or even seconds. Those within teams dedicated to checking and testing the work of their colleagues would also be held accountable if they let through products found to be faulty on later tests. In one company, even after all the in-process and final tests, samples of goods which have been packaged are stripped back down and retested: any rework found necessary (which by this stage is quite rare) has to be carried out *by the people who caused the defect on the same day*.

The ability to speedily take corrective action in the case of negative divergences from quality and other targets, and to incorporate savings in the case of positive divergences, is of course dependent on a high degree of visibility of production processes and close monitoring – in other words, an efficient system of surveillance.[9] 'Visible management' and 'visible controls' were terms in popular use at several companies, these being achieved in part by tight control over work-in-progress (so that any problems come to light quickly, rather than being hidden for days or weeks in buffer stocks), and also by simple and clear displays of targets, output and defects. In 19 out of 22 companies performances against target were displayed at the level of the team, section or department, and in 14 cases the displays were updated at least hourly. In some cases output against targets was displayed in real time following final electronic and visual quality checks, so that, as one production manager put it, 'even our managing director knows how we're doing at a glance'. An example of a performance chart is provided in Figure 4.1.

Hourly Production Record														
	Date:													
Time	7.00	8.00	9.00	10.00	11.00	12.00 noon	1.00	2.00	3.00	4.00	5.00	6.00	7.00	8.00
Target (cumulative)	452	904	1356	1808	2185	2637	3089	3541	3993	4445	4897	5349	5726	6175
Actual (cumulative)														
Difference														
Actual quantity produced during hour														
Rejects this hour														
Cumulative rejects														
Pallet number														
Quantity on pallet														
Cumulative production														
Manufacturing														Form: MAN 08

Figure 4.1 Hourly production record

Work organization and work discipline

Work in Japanese manufacturing transplants in Wales is characterized by team organization, typically based around production lines dedicated to the production of a component family or the final assembly of a family of products. Teams vary in size, but most often will consist of 15 to 30 employees, and will include inspectors and technicians, as well as operators under the control of a team leader, with a small number of multi-skilled 'floats'. Teams have their own responsibility for monitoring, documenting and displaying their productivity and quality performances against targets set by industrial engineers and production managers.

Tasks carried out by individual operators – especially in the dominant electronics plants – are mostly short cycle, consisting of a sequence of operations which will take around 30 seconds as the component or product being assembled moves past on the line. Operators are generally expected to be able to perform more than one task, to allow for flexible and efficient labour deployment in the face of absences and model or demand changes: in some companies boards adjacent to production lines indicate the jobs each individual in the team is capable of performing, simplifying the team leader's role in task allocation on a day to day or week by week basis. Flexibility is not always easy to achieve, although not because of worker resistance. One manager commented that:

> Ideally, we like each operator to be able to do five jobs, but this is difficult to achieve because of labour turnover and in periods of production pressure . . . [But] thirty per cent of operators have been with us five years plus, and these are very flexible people.

The reality in most companies was a limited amount of job rotation – sometimes none – for most operators, but a high degree of flexible deployment for some of the more experienced operators, and especially for floats.

If a team member is late or absent the team leader reallocates tasks, or might ask a float to fill in for the absentee: floats are expected to be capable of performing most or all of the tasks on the line. Because of the float's other responsibilities, however, the preference is for floats to fill in only for brief periods. One of the float's responsibilities is typically to document productivity and quality information and keep performance displays up to date. As described above, this task is undertaken carefully and the results taken seriously. In one company team leaders visited the production office several times a day to write their team's performances on a large white board. A green pen is used for positive variances (ahead of target) and red for negative (behind target). The production manager joked that 'it's a great motivator. I can see at a glance if they pick up the red pen so I can chuck the board duster at them.'

Joking apart, the production manager was illustrating a serious point about work motivation and discipline in Japanese transplants: both teams and individual operators are effectively disciplined on a day to day (or literally hour to hour or minute to minute) basis through 'visible management' and 'short feedback loops'. As one manager commented, 'each individual knows if she's made a fault we'll know it's her'. He went on

> We have status charts so we know exactly who was on the job when. Within a few hours at most we know who's made a mistake, and take immediate action. Mount line supervisors visit the main lines at least every hour to collect defect information and they use this to update fault sheets and they feed it straight back to the individual. We often bring operators to the main line to show them what they did wrong.

Of course, the certain knowledge on the part of operators that any mistake they make will be traced back to them, and speedily, makes it less likely that they will make mistakes in the first place. Where mistakes are traced back the cause of the problem is carefully established, and when it is certain that the fault lies with the operator rather than, say, a machine or faulty materials, this fact is recorded. In some companies individual quality performances are publicly displayed, and in most there is a display for the team's performance. Unacceptable quality performances by individuals, then, might be made public, arguably a sanction in itself; records of performance against targets might also feed into appraisals (where companies use them) and therefore affect salary and promotion prospects. Ultimately, if retraining or redeployment to another part of the factory fails to result in acceptable standards, the employee will be dismissed. On the whole, our impression was that whilst employee performances were very closely policed, management would also put a serious effort into improving individuals' capabilities: unacceptable performances were quickly noted and the person made aware of the fact, but a whole range of measures such as counselling, retraining and redeployment were attempted before dismissal – discipline was corrective rather than merely punitive. One manager put it as follows: 'Our preferred style is one of persuasion, involvement, encouragement: the iron fist in the velvet glove.'

Because of the tight staffing policies described above, it is not surprising that strict discipline also applies to time-keeping and absence. One manager pointed out that:

> When people start they show difficulties over attendance. We need 100 per cent attendance. The average (absentee rate) is now around three per cent . . . this compares with an average for the locality of six or seven per cent. We've had to dismiss people for poor attendance.

Employees are made aware that absence or lateness affects other team members: one company's employee handbook states that:

> Working with [us] means working as a member of a team and any lateness or absence on your part will not only interrupt the work of your team but will also affect production and throw added work on other company members . . . In most cases, these [absence] records have been achieved because the people concerned feel a responsibility towards the company and their colleagues and are proud of the standards they have achieved.

In five companies we visited the attempt to utilize peer pressures to control absence and lateness was heightened by publicly displaying the names of absentees, sometimes with the recorded reason for their absence. In one joint-venture company such public displays were avoided because, according to one manager, 'that would be the equivalent of the stocks'. In common with all the companies we visited, however, detailed individual absence and lateness records were kept and return-to-work interviews were carried out by team leaders as a matter of company policy. A manager in one company which did not enforce a policy on public displays of absence commented:

> Some section leaders display the chart, some don't. It's up to them. These figures are published every day for managers as well, and they're always an important item at the daily production meeting. We're very strict on absence and lateness, and this is a very important point during probation. Return-to-work counselling is automatic.

The return-to-work interview is typically the first step in a strict disciplinary system. Systems and procedures vary between companies, but it is not unusual for two separate absences within a three month period to lead to a warning and probation, with dismissal the eventual result if the record is not improved.[10] Illness is not necessarily viewed as a good excuse. A document given all employees by one company reads:

> Submission of a medical statement, although a useful piece of information, is not always regarded by the company as sufficient justification for accepting your absence . . . although due note will be taken of the opinion of your own doctor, the final decision on your suitability for continued employment shall rest with the company.

In some companies supervisors and managers were encouraged to maintain contact by telephone or occasional home visits with those absent for prolonged periods, and in one company a system whereby managers would make random visits to the homes of even short-term absentees to check that their declared reason for absence was genuine was being instituted. Such activities, in some companies spelled out in supervisors' procedure manuals, were considered a good deterrent.

Not surprisingly, we documented remarkably low absence levels. Excluding planned absence (holidays, etc.) the lowest was 0.6 per cent and the highest 7 per cent – the latter in a newly established joint-venture company. The average was 3.9 per cent.

'Bell-to-bell' working, which requires employees to be at the production line for every minute of the official working times, is commonly practised. One company expresses its requirements in great detail to its employees as follows:

> Normal working hours are 0745 hours until 1700 hours Monday to Thursday; 0745 hours until 1435 hours Friday.
>
> At the commencement of each working day, the first bell will sound at 0742, at which time employees should make their way to work

stations, ready to commence work on the second bell, at 0745 hours. The same principle also applies to tea and lunch breaks, i.e. employees should make their way to their work stations on hearing the first bell.

Tea and lunch breaks are staggered as follows:

	Tea break	1st bell	2nd bell	Lunch	1st bell	2nd bell	Tea break	1st bell	2nd bell
1st break	0945	0957	1000	1150	1222	1225	1450	1457	1500
2nd break	1015	1027	1030	1235	1307	1310	1510	1517	1520

Strict discipline applies to many other areas beyond absence, lateness and time-keeping. Smoking, eating and drinking are strictly banned from production areas, and there are strictly enforced rules on issues such as housekeeping, health and safety, theft, drugs, etc.

Tony Pegge, then Personnel Executive at Hitachi in Hirwaun, provides a stark account of the differences between standards of discipline in 'a typical South Wales Valleys factory' – the GEC television factory before 1984 – and those in a Japanese-owned factory – the same factory when Hitachi took complete control.[11] He comments:

> We have stopped people smoking inside the factory, which they have done since 1949. We have said 'we are an electronics factory and the rule, when you come back on the 6th August into our new agreement, will be that when you go through the doors of the factory you don't smoke'.
>
> We have stopped people eating their lunches from the top of the television sets. They used to have bacon, egg and beans on top of the television sets – which appalled the Japanese! We said to them 'From the 6th August the factory is where you work, the restaurant is where you eat'. We have stopped drinking at the workplace as well.

On working time, Pegge further comments:

> Hitachi wanted all 39 hours of production time to be just that. They wanted all 'washing up' times to disappear. That involved three minute allowances at the start of the morning, lunch and afternoon breaks and at finish time. Our people said . . . 'we are ready to give up all of the first three minutes. We want to finish at 4.27. We need that three minutes to be washing up, to get clean to go home on the buses'.

> Hitachi thought that was appalling . . . the way in which people would not see that an extra 180 seconds of production was a certain number of television sets. . . . But they decided at the end of the day [to relent].

In summary, work in Japanese transplant factories is characterized by teams with a higher degree of responsibility which are more self-contained than is the case in traditional British factories. At the same time, Japanese companies do base their operations on production-line principles, and the obsession with work-cycle times and the efficiencies arising from industrial engineering and detailed job measurements suggests a degree of continuity with, certainly not a complete break from, Taylorist or Fordist principles. Similarly, although a degree of job rotation and flexible labour deployment is practised, much of the work carried out is short-cycle and repetitive. Where Japanese transplants do stand out as being very different is with regard to waste elimination through *kaizen* or 'continuous improvement', and to surveillance and discipline through 'quality control'. Working in a Japanese transplant means accepting there will be little in the way of idle time or slack labour, and submitting to a strict system of discipline in which any mistake or misdemeanour will be recorded and action taken.

One manager we interviewed commented that 'I've visited Japan and we're very successful by their standards. Ours talk more than they do but other than that we work Japanese-style.' Positive comments about the Welsh workforce were common amongst other interviewees, confirming statements occasionally made in the press by Japanese senior managers about local workforce qualities. The President of Matsushita, explaining the reasons for the establishment of a third Welsh plant in 1988, went so far as to say that the company 'knew that workers in Wales are extremely good and in fact seem to have much in common with Japanese. This was . . . a major decision-making factor for selecting Port Talbot.'[12]

However, we would argue that any suggestion of cultural similarity between Japanese and Welsh workers be treated with extreme caution. As we have shown, Welsh workers 'working Japanese-style' are doing so under a strict system of discipline which inevitably means sanctions if they fail to do so. Further, Japanese-style work practices have been introduced into Wales mostly on greenfield sites and mostly since the late 1970s in a context of economic decline and high unemployment. Arguably, the context has been favourable to the introduction of radically new work practices, underpinned by supportive personnel and industrial-relations systems (described in Chapters 5 and 6). Most importantly, although work practices appear to be transferable, the transfer of a 'work ethic' is less easily identified. One Japanese director, when asked to explain the lower productivity performance of the Welsh compared with the Japanese sister plant, commented to us that

> it's the mentality of the Japanese people. There, when the buzzer goes off at 12 o'clock for lunch or five o'clock for shift end, they do the job until they've finished it. Here they stop. The attitude to work is different.

For the purposes of this book we will neither make assumptions about, nor comparisons between, the attitudes of Welsh and Japanese workers; nor will we compare work ethics in the two countries.[13] The Welsh workforce, on our own evidence and according to other accounts, has adapted with remarkably little resistance or complaint to a Japanese style of working, but we believe this can be explained by reference to personnel and industrial relations practices, which are described in Chapters 5 and 6.

The shopfloor hierarchy

A range of terms are used to describe the shopfloor hierarchy in Japanese transplants. In this book we have generally used the terms 'operator', 'float', 'team leader', 'supervisor' and 'production manager'.

Immediately above the operator is the float, sometimes called the 'leading hand', 'senior operator' or 'group leader'. Anything between 1 to 6 and 1 to 16 operators could be 'floats'. In most cases the term 'float' probably derives from the notion of 'floating labour', which has traditionally been used in Western organizations to fill in for absentees, late-comers, early-leavers, and toilet-goers, so that the pace of the production line can be maintained. Indeed, such a role characterizes the work of floats in Japanese transplant companies, who also have to fill in when operators are taken for counselling, or to their customer team or final inspection area when it is deemed necessary to give them a practical demonstration of the problems they are causing. It is from those operators found practically capable of reliably performing most of the tasks within a team that floats are selected; not surprisingly virtually all floats are internally promoted.

However, the role of the float is not just to 'fill in' when the need arises (this would represent human 'waste' and a 'slack' system of production).[14] The float's flexibility typically extends beyond a set of operator tasks to include the delivery of materials to the line, the on-the-job training of new operators or those operators being rotated, and the collection, recording and display of information, quality information in particular, from test areas or from customer teams. In these latter regards the float is effectively taking on tasks which, if a strict division of labour was observed, would be the preserve of materials handlers, personnel trainers and quality specialists.

Not surprisingly, and again almost invariably - except for those companies starting up or suddenly expanding with the addition of new plant - team leaders are selected from floats. Typically, they are responsible for 30–40 employees. The team leader is the nearest equivalent to the old British foreman, and in addition to the skills in which the float is trained, is expected to have leadership qualities. One manager commented that:

> The supervisor in British industry had degenerated into a 'go-for' . . . here the [team leader] is responsible for productivity, materials, quality control, as well as motivation of his or her group.

Team leaders are held accountable for team performance, which is sytematically compared with the performances of other teams within the company and sometimes across group companies around the world. Their work is intensive and potentially stressful. Minimally, in addition to the above responsibilities, they have to communicate targets and standards (determined from above) via team briefings, and to counsel 'problem' employees. Sometimes they are also involved in final decisions on selection of employees into their team, and where appraisal systems are in place, they are expected to make judgements which will influence or determine the fate of their team members.

Team leaders are expected to develop good relationships with their team members, with their supervisors and with fellow team leaders, and there is an emphasis on face to face communication. In line with such an emphasis (and also in line, perhaps, with the emphasis on 'visible management') team leaders' desks, filing cabinets, computer terminals, etc., are not shut behind office doors, but typically are found adjacent to or at the end of production lines. The value of good communications and visible management can be seen when there is any production problem – the team leader is likely to be on the spot – and at the start of shifts when the leaders hold discussions with each other and with their floats and their supervisors over precise staffing arrangements in the light of the day's targets and the labour available. At the same time, in some areas, team leaders are expected to carefully follow detailed rules and procedures. This applies particularly to production and quality monitoring, to dealing with time-keeping and absence problems, and to the provision of detailed information to senior production and personnel staff.[15] The effect is that, whilst team leaders' responsibilities are broad, their work and their performance, like that of their individual team members, is closely scrutinized.

Peter Wickens, referring to the Nissan plant in Sunderland, suggests their team leader system almost represents 'a return to the old style foreman before the specialists took away and diminished many of his tasks'.[16] To a degree this comment rang true for the team leader role in Japanese transplants in Wales, but it is important not to confuse task variety with autonomy: team leaders were responsible for carrying out a range of tasks which might belong to specialists or managers in non-Japanese organizations, but in many areas their roles were bureaucratically prescribed, their targets were set from above, and their performance was closely monitored. The effect, arguably, is the tightening of senior management control over detailed operations, for this becomes direct via the team leader rather than through a great army of bureaucrats and specialists.

Most companies had a policy of internal promotion above the level of team leader, and in some of the longer established Japanese transplants in Wales we interviewed production supervisors and managers who had worked their way up from the shopfloor.[17] In most cases, however, those staff above team leader level had been carefully recruited externally. The qualities sought of managers were a combination of professional skills, together with a willingness to work flexibly, to work in a team, and with a commitment to continuous improvement. If anything, managerial work was even more demanding than that of floats or team leaders. One manager commented that 'a good manager in a Japanese company has got to be able to combine professionalism with giving his life to the company.'

Another said that, compared with his previous work experience in British companies, working in a Japanese transplant was

> much busier, much more expected of you, much more get the job done . . . much longer hours than anywhere else I've seen . . . with the Japanese you've literally got to kick them out and tell them to go home.

One manager said his recent heart attack was probably related to long hours and job stress.[18] These observations equate with the numerical evidence we gathered on working hours, which (by managers' subjective estimates and excluding homework) averaged 51 per week across all companies for British managers, and 61 for Japanese managers: one large company, we were told, had a Japanese union representative 'who goes around wearing a red armband telling his people "please go home"'. The company's corporate policy was to establish a 1,800 hour year,[19] but it was recognized that implementation would be a long and difficult process.

In most cases the managing director of the transplant operation is Japanese, and while other senior positions are often staffed by British managers, there is likely to be at least a handful of Japanese support staff or 'advisers' who help maintain the link with Japan. A recent letter to *The Financial Times* from an ex-Sony engineer complained of the 'frustration' felt by local staff 'because of the feeling of constantly having their shoulders looked over and having to justify their actions to their [Japanese] shadows'.[20] Unfortunately, whether such frustration is widespread is not a question we can answer from our own research endeavours. Apart from rare exceptions in a few companies for the managing director, or for the personnel manager on the grounds of confidentiality, offices are open plan. This encourages a high level of face to face communication which, combined with 'shadowing', means that managerial work, like that on the shopfloor, is characterized by a degree of 'visibility'.

The degree of control and direction from head office in Japan was often described to us as 'loose' and many managers said the transplant operation had a high degree of autonomy. However, 'our fax machine is a hot machine' and 'our telephone bill is horrific' were popular comments, and companies were expected to report regularly with a whole range of business ratios and other performance indicators. Performance comparisons among plants producing similar products across the world were sometimes systematically conducted, and managers would often visit Japan to learn lessons about how things are done there. British senior managers were sometimes puzzled at the absence of detailed instructions from Japan: one director commented that 'after three and a half years (of working here) I still don't know the decision-making system'. However, expectations of a high performance and the continuous improvement of performance certainly were successfully communicated, and these translated into dedication, a strong task orientation and attention to detail amongst local managers.

FIVE

Personnel Management

In Japan core workers in large companies often enjoy lifetime employment, seniority-based pay and promotion, and extensive company welfare provision.[1] Peripheral workers - part-time and temporary workers in large companies and most of those employed in small companies - on the other hand are less likely to enjoy welfare benefits and their jobs are insecure. It is clear that the employment contract between Welsh employee and Japanese transplant company does not parallel the core worker model in Japan.[2] None the less, personnel management systems and practices appear to have been designed in a manner which leads to an acceptance of the tight shopfloor discipline and flexible labour deployment described in Chapter 4.[3]

Of course, Japanese companies entering Wales have been aided in their ability to establish new working practices in a context, in the 1980s and into the 1990s, of an abundant supply of readily available labour. As well as being highly selective of those candidates most likely to fit the company culture, however, induction, training, appraisal, payment and communications systems all help create a situation supportive of an efficient deployment of labour.

Selection

The selection of staff in Japanese companies in Wales is a thorough process. According to one personnel manager, 'Compared with other companies in Wales our recruitment process is much longer, much more people involved, much more discussion.' The following summarizes an account by a personnel manager at another company. After gathering application forms a 'first cut' is made on the basis of previous experience (factory experience is viewed positively), education and length of service in previous employment (job-hopping is viewed unfavourably). Those who pass the first cut are invited to the factory to take a test consisting of arithmetic, logic and basic operator abilities (e.g. reject calculations); the final part of the test comprises a moral question which 'gives us a feel for their integrity'. Those who pass the test are interviewed by personnel staff for a minimum of half an hour, the interview being structured around the application form and the moral question. The personnel department makes a decision on an individual's suitability for employment and writes a report, but then a second interview by the team leader for whom the candidate would work is undertaken while the applicant is being shown around the factory: this is considered an opportunity to assess the candidate's reaction to seeing life on the shopfloor, and also to give the candidates the opportunity to assess whether they really wish to work there. The team leader writes a short report, and in fact has the right of veto over the personnel department's decision. The managing director examines all the paperwork, and is willing to argue against recommendations, but in the end accepts the decisions of personnel staff and team leaders. A previous Japanese managing director refused to accept any selection decisions where the candidate was deemed to be fat (height–weight ratios were measured); but after six months he relented when British personnel staff finally persuaded him that fat people were not necessarily lazy.

Apart from the use, for a short period, of height–weight ratios as a selection criterion, the above account might be considered typical. As well as the length of the procedure and the number of staff involved, two aspects are worth pointing out. First, the immediate superior – the team leader in the case of operator recruitment – has an involvement in the selection process. This is the case for most Japanese companies in Wales, and is one of the ways in which team leaders have broader responsibilities than might be typical of the British foreman. It is also, arguably, a means of heightening the accountability of the team leader: if new recruits perform poorly, and team performance suffers as a consequence, the team leader cannot simply blame the personnel department for providing her or him with poor (human) materials to work with. Secondly, the candidates, in this case by being shown around the shopfloor, are being given the opportunity to see at first hand what work will be like, to ask questions, and to deselect themselves if they do not like what they see. In being open with potential employees, the company is effectively beginning the process of workforce socialization before new employees have taken their places on the line. Some companies extend the opportunity for deselection by inviting employees to leave should they so desire at the end of an induction programme lasting several days. Making candidates feel they have participated in the selection process, as well as setting clear expectations and priming employees for their new roles, also reduces the likelihood of very costly high staff turnover over the first weeks and months of employment – those employees who would have left on the grounds that 'I wouldn't have come to work here if I had known' will ideally have already deselected themselves.

In a very real sense the selection process in all the Japanese companies in Wales which we studied continued for thirteen weeks from the commencement of employment up to the end of a probationary period. All companies reserved the right not to confirm employment at the end of this period, and 5 companies told us that probation was systematically used in selection. A manager at one company said that at the selection interview 'we're looking for a spark of sensibility and a keenness to work', but that it was during the three-month probation that 'we sort the wheat from the chaff'. At another company, the three month selection process was unambiguously spelled out in a document given to all newly recruited employees:

> On joining the company, you will be subject to an initial probationary period of 13 weeks. During this time, your manager will assess your fitness, capabilities, attitudes and potential, the company will take up references and you can decide if this is the type of work you want to do. If the company finds everything is satisfactory and you like working with us, at the end of the 13 week period, you will be confirmed as a company member. If during this period your performance is unsatisfactory, your employment will be terminated or in certain circumstances the probationary period may be extended.

As can be seen from Table 5.1, Japanese companies place an emphasis on attitudes in recruitment. This fits with the desire to

Dexterity, concentration	7
Past attendance and time-keeping record	10
Attitude to flexible working, quality	12
Attitude to teamwork	4
Stable domestic background	4
Enthusiasm, ambition	4
Work experience	9
Education, intelligence	7

Table 5.1: *Selection criteria for operators in Japanese companies in Wales (N = 22)*
Source: Authors' Survey, 1992.

recruit workers who will be willing to work flexibly and accept Japanese work practices.

Sometimes held as a criticism against Japanese employment practices in Wales during the 1980s, Japanese companies came to have a reputation for recruiting school leavers with no previous work experience, no practical knowledge of trade union activities, and most importantly, untainted with 'bad habits' picked up from working with British companies. Orion's managing director in 1988 was quoted as saying that

> most of our workforce are relatively young, so there are lots of benefits here. They easily adapt to changing conditions, and because some come straight from school, training and re-training is far easier with them.[4]

A production manager at another company in interview with the authors made a comment echoing the same sentiment: 'You need people not trained in the bad habits of British industry. Our work-force is young and provided you talk to them and involve them they're very amenable to change.'

However as shown earlier, we documented a shift away from targeting school leavers in recruitment over the last few years. Six companies had deliberately shifted recruitment strategy because of problems of labour turnover, absence and indiscipline. One manager commented:

> In the past we tended to take on young females. Now we go for a good age mix; an older element is important, this has helped stabilize the

workforce. We look for a stable domestic background, and if they have a financial commitment that's good.

Three companies which had invested in the late 1980s had deliberately avoided a heavy reliance on school leavers from start up because of stories they had heard from longer established inward investors. According to one manager:

> We knew that other Japanese companies had had difficulties with school leavers, so we avoided a reliance on these from the beginning. Many of our operators had had four or five jobs over the last few years because of firms opening and closing in the area. They appreciate the stability and open communications here. Most of our employees have had some factory experience. The average age is 27.

Annual turnover rates at the time of our study (early 1992) varied between a low of 1 per cent and a high of 32 per cent per year, averaging 8.2 per cent. In most companies these figures were reduced sharply from 1989–90 and 1990–91 because of the effects of the recession and rising unemployment in Wales, although some companies reckoned the shift in selection strategy towards candidates with 'stable domestic backgrounds' and 'financial commitments' was also a factor.

Hence, whilst flexibility, a willingness to change jobs, and a positive attitude to training and retraining are desirable qualities, so are 'reliability', 'attendance', and an ability 'to do a line job for eight hours a day', as one manager put it. Another said, 'the Japanese have often been surprised at the lack of loyalty and commitment to the company'. It is in the light of the attempt to develop *all* these qualities among the workforce that Japanese transplants in Wales continue to refine their selection procedures.

Japanese companies in Wales may not go to the length of hiring private detectives to check for undesirable qualities or social connections, as they are reported to do in Japan,[5] but the time and care taken over selection is an outstanding feature of personnel management in Japanese transplants in Wales.[6]

The same might be said of induction programmes. In Japan, a ten day induction, involving group residence, team activities, physical exercise and indoctrination sessions, typically ends with new entrants reading a speech pledging their best efforts to the company.[7] In Wales, transplant companies do not behave towards new recruits in a manner we might feel is more appropriate for girl guides or boy scouts,[8] but initial socialization is taken seriously.

Induction, training and career management

Formal inductions were carried out in all the Japanese plants in Wales we visited, the length varying from a brief one and a half days to a lengthy two weeks, the average being around three and a half days. The formal induction typically provides recruits with an overview of the company, company history and philosophy, company rules and discipline, etc. It is also an opportunity to impress on recruits the importance of teamwork, flexibility, quality consciousness and the desire for continuous improvement. Employee handbooks documenting company rules and grievance and discipline procedures are usually given out. (In at least 8 companies the induction also includes an address to the recruits by a trade union representative - company acceptance or encouragement of trade union membership is a point taken up in the next chapter).

Formal induction is immediately followed by on-the-job training for operators. Typically, this consists of the operator taking a place on the line next to an experienced operator or float for coaching. Starting with, say, half a task, the operator is expected to gradually build up speed over a period of a few days or a week, until she/he can cope with a full task at full line speed. Training in more than one task was provided in virtually all companies, and the close monitoring of probationers is used to establish in which type of job they will best fit, as well as their general suitability for employment. Whilst in none of the companies we visited was there any direct link between skills acquired and the rate of pay, skills acquisition was sometimes a necessary, but not sufficient, condition for a higher grade, and those employees willing and capable of achieving competence in several jobs, and having good time-keeping and attendance records, would be likely, within two to three years, to be promoted to the position of float with a higher pay grade.

Generally speaking, there is a strong training emphasis in Japanese companies in Wales, mostly on-the-job and in-house for operators. The skills developed are company-specific and would not be readily transferred to other companies, though many companies do have a policy of sponsoring any employee to do a course of their choosing outside working hours if it can be shown the skills developed could have some value to the company. One company stood out in having around 100 employees presently on four-year apprenticeships, consisting of one year full-time at college followed by three years work experience with one day per week in college. The company was one of five Welsh companies to win a National Training Award in 1989.

The latter company being one of a small number of exceptions, most companies did not have career management systems, or to be more accurate, the career management system of the parent corporation did not embrace the Welsh transplant. In the United States considerable disgruntlement on the part of American managers in Japanese companies over the lack of career prospects has been documented.[9] Similarly, referring to Hitachi in Hirwaun, Tony Pegge has commented that

> It seems that the Japanese respect age and service and loyalty more than incisiveness, and that certainly is a frustration.[10]

In one long established company in Wales a manager commented that

> in the early days length of service and age were important, but we've gradually broken that down. We actually lost some key staff in the early 1980s because of career frustrations. We had to persuade Japanese managers that we're in the UK not Japan.

However, in Wales in most companies we did not detect particularly high levels of career dissatisfaction among managers, although the relative recency of Japanese inward investment there as compared with that in the USA, combined with rapid growth and, therefore, a good deal of internal promotion prospects during the 1980s, may, in part, account for this. The steady expansion, which for the great majority of companies has followed the initial investment, has accommodated many British managers' career ambitions: whether the expectations of rapid career progression will continue to be met may depend in part on the extent of further expansion, and also the extent to which, as one manager put it, 'we can convince the Japanese that we are operating in Wales, not Japan'.

Appraisals

One of the less popularly known facts of employment in Japan is the importance of personal appraisal. Most large companies use a form of personal assessment known as *satei*, which influences both the rate of promotion and the level of pay. According to Endo[11] the appraisal, based on recent performance and subjective assessments of personality and behaviour by the immediate superior, leads to an acceptance of managerial prerogatives, under-reporting of working hours, and a refusal to apply for the full paid holiday entitlement. Whilst appraisal systems grew in popularity in Britain independently of, and prior to, the Japanese presence, they have largely been restricted to managerial and white-collar staffs, and the results of appraisals have been decoupled from pay and promotion considerations: in other words, appraisals in Britain have been 'developmental' rather than 'judgemental' in nature. Whilst the extent to which the appraisal systems in Japanese transplants in Wales were designed or influenced by parent companies remains unclear, the judgemental emphasis is apparent.[12] Table 5.2 shows the extent to which appraisals are used, and who is subject to appraisal. Only very small, or newly established, companies do not have an appraisal system. In 11 companies all employees were subject to appraisal, with another 2 planning appraisals for all.

In 3 of the 5 cases where appraisals were restricted to management and administrative staffs, this was because, as one manager put it, 'if we tried to introduce operator appraisal we'd have a serious problem with the union'. Given the general trade union

		Yearly	*Twice yearly*
All employees	11	6	5
Management/Administration only	5	4	1
Probationers only	2	At end of probation period	
System planned	2		
No appraisal	3		

Table 5.2: *Use and frequency of appraisals in Japanese companies in Wales (N = 23)*
Source: Authors' Survey, 1992.

PERFORMANCE ASSESSMENT FORM

NAME	EMPLOYEE NO	DATE OF BIRTH
JOB TITLE	SECTION/LINE	
DATE JOINED	DATE OF EXPIRY OF PROBATION PERIOD	

	EX	VG	G	F	P
1. Attendance, including late arrivals, early leavings					
2. Leaving place of work without permission, time wasting					
3. Adherence to Company rules and Supervisor's instructions					
4. Willingness to accept allocated tasks					
5. Ability to work without disturbing other people					
6. Speed of work					
7. Initiative and interest in understanding the needs of the job					
8. Quality of workmanship and contribution to team effort					
9. Reports and information (where necessary) punctually given to supervisor					
10. Extent of skills acquired during probation period					
TOTAL (%)					

	MONTH 1	MONTH 2	MONTH 3	TOTAL
ABSENCE/ SICK LEAVE	U SL	U SL	U SL	U SL
LATE ARRIVING/ EARLY LEAVING	LA EL	LA EL	LA EL	LA EL
ASSESSOR'S COMMENTS				
SECTION HEAD'S COMMENTS				

Signed .... Date....................
(Assessor)

....
(Section Head)

Employee's Signature ....

Figure 5.1 Probationers' personal assessment form

acceptance of, if not enthusiasm for, operator appraisal in most Japanese transplants, such a comment may appear bizarre. However, 2 of the 3 companies which appeared to fear union disgruntlement were established prior to the 1980s when, arguably, it was more difficult to treat employees on an individual as opposed to a collective basis. That individual appraisal is now virtually taken for granted in Japanese transplants may say as much about the general reassertion of managerial prerogatives in Britain as it does about Japanese management styles. An additional reason given for not appraising operators was that this could be demotivating and discourage teamwork. The companies which did use personal appraisals – i.e. most – reported no union objections, let alone union resistance, and generally they felt that the appraisal system was supportive of the work practices they wished to encourage. Certainly the appraisal criteria, like selection criteria, focused on those desirable employee attributes such as flexibility, teamwork and responsibility. In addition, measures such as quality performance and, of course, attendance and time-keeping, were used to inform the result.

Most often the appraisal is carried out by the immediate superior – the team leader in the case of operators. In most cases employees are graded on a scale against the range of desirable attributes, some of which can be objectively ascertained from quality, attendance and other records, and others such as 'attitude to work' and 'teamwork ability' being dependent on the subjective judgement of the superior. Examples of personal assessment forms are provided in Figures 5.1 (for probationers) and 5.2 (for all permanent employees).

In one company, 'a link between money and appraisal is deliberately avoided because it doesn't fit with developmental purposes'.

Promotion	12
Pay	9
Identification of training needs	8
Selection (from probationer to permanent)	5
Redundancies	1

Table 5.3: *Uses of operator appraisal results in Japanese Companies in Wales (N = 13)*
Source: Authors' Survey, 1992.
Note: The thirteen cases in this table include two companies which plan to introduce appraisals in the near future.

1. GENERAL SKILLS

Comment on specific strengths/weaknesses, achievements etc. INDICATE IF FACTOR IS NOT APPLICABLE

1. JOB KNOWLEDGE

Knows fully all aspects	Acceptable job knowledge	Below required level but progressing well	Below required level but not progressing well
☐	☐	☐	☐

2. QUALITY OF WORK

Consistent highest quality in all aspects	Good in most aspects	Of varying quality	Not acceptable
☐	☐	☐	☐

3. COMMUNICATIONS—WRITTEN & VERBAL

An outstanding and effective communicator	Communicates proficiently	Needs to improve	Does not communicate—significant change needed
☐	☐	☐	☐

4. SAFETY HOUSEKEEPING

Always maintaining highest standards in all aspects of work	Aware of need and tries hard	Does not pay sufficient attention	Poor attitude to safety/ housekeeping
☐	☐	☐	☐

5. PROBLEM SOLVING

Outstanding	Generally very good	Fully acceptable	Has difficulty	Usually not able to think through problems
☐	☐	☐	☐	☐

6. EFFECTIVENESS & APPLICATION

Excellent	Above average	Average	Below average
☐	☐	☐	☐

7. FLEXIBILITY

Rigid and inflexible	Not very flexible	Acceptable flexibility	Welcomes new methods and tasks	Constantly seeking to increase personal flexibility
☐	☐	☐	☐	☐

8. TEAMWORKING

Always seeks to involve others	Works well as a team member	Makes good effort to be a team worker	Dislikes team working	A total loner
☐	☐	☐	☐	☐

9. ATTENDANCE

100% attendance	Only absent when beyond control	Some improvement possible	Has been criticized for attendance
☐	☐	☐	☐

10. TIME-KEEPING

100% time-keeping never late	Only late when beyond control	Some improvement possible	Has been criticized for time-keeping
☐	☐	☐	☐

Figure 5.2 Permanent employees' personal assessment form

2. SPECIFIC SKILLS

1. CREATIVITY/INITIATIVE

Dislikes change	Does not initiate	Welcomes new initiatives	Regularly seeks improvements	Too ready to introduce change
☐	☐	☐	☐	☐

2. LEADERSHIP

An outstanding leader	Leads well on most occasions	Does lead at appropriate times	Does not normally lead	Not at all a leader
☐	☐	☐	☐	☐

3. PLANNING OF WORK

Superbly organized	Generally well organized	Adequate under supervision	Inadequate planning
☐	☐	☐	☐

4. QUALITY OF DECISIONS

Makes frequent errors	Mostly correct	Clear and always correct	Avoids making decisions
☐	☐	☐	☐

5. INTERPERSONAL SKILLS

Sensitive and constructive	Tries hard to maintain good working relationships	Some improvement possible	Poor feedback, and relationship with other members
☐	☐	☐	☐

6. PERSONAL COMMITMENT

Positive resilient and adaptable	Generally good and constructive approach	Does not normally positively contribute	Definitely lacking in any personal commitment
☐	☐	☐	☐

7. MOTIVATION OF STAFF

Outstanding and effective motivator	Motivates to the best of their ability	Unable to successfully motivate	Poor attitude to staff motivation
☐	☐	☐	☐

3. APPRAISER COMMENTS

Figure 5.2 continued

4. APPRAISEE COMMENTS

APPRAISER .... DATED..............

APPRAISEE .... DATED..............

5. COMMENTS BY SENIOR REPORTING MANAGER

SIGNED .... DATED..............

Figure 5.2 continued

This was not generally the case, however. For the 13 companies applying or planning to apply personal appraisal to operators, the uses of results are indicated in Table 5.3.

As can be seen in Table 5.3, whilst 'developmental' purposes were important ('identification of training needs') 'judgemental' aspects predominated ('promotion', 'pay'). In one company the appraisal system was used in favour of the 'last in first out' (LIFO) convention when redundancies had to be meted out, perhaps the ultimate judgemental use of an appraisal scheme. Redundancies in Japanese companies in Wales – and Britain as a whole – have been extremely rare, so generalization is difficult, but the evidence does not suggest that length of service or loyalty necessarily take precedence. Tony Pegge reported that at Hitachi in 1984:

> The Japanese thought that to go for selective redundancy would be a way of removing a lot of the people who were non-performers who could be located by a little matrix of efficiency, rejects, attendance, and so on.[13]

Pegge said that LIFO was chosen, but only because enough public attention had already been drawn to the company due to its radical approach to industrial relations (see next chapter). The contemplated surgical removal of 500 'non-performers' in this case, and their actual removal in another case, point up the question of whether Welsh workers in Japanese transplants are 'core' or 'peripheral' workers. Certainly, the whole approach to appraisal for lower grades of staff in many companies fits uneasily with notions of seniority and lifetime employment.

Rewards

Of the 9 cases where operators' pay was affected by the results of appraisals, in 5 the result influenced the pay grade within a job class (in theory the pay grade could go down as well as up, but in practice rarely did so), in 2 the result determined bonus payments, and in 2 the negotiated annual salary rise was not paid to individuals uniformly, but depended on the appraisal result (for instance, if the negotiated overall rise was, say, 6 per cent, an individual employee might receive anything between 3 and 9 per cent, depending on the appraisal). Table 5.4 shows other influences on levels of pay received by operators.

The pay differentials among employees in the same job class resulting from appraisals, length of service and attendance were generally quite small. The largest such differential we documented was an appraisal-determined 23 per cent, and less than 10 per cent was typical. Positive motivational effects were none the less emphasized by managers. It is also worth mentioning the apparent

Basic only	5
Appraisal	9
Seniority	4
Profit sharing	1
Plant-wide bonus	2
Attendance bonus	6

Table 5.4: *Influences on operator pay in Japanese companies in Wales (N = 21)*
Source: Authors' Survey, 1992.

importance given to symbolic rewards within the workplace, which were frequently given to teams, and occasionally individuals. Announcements on posters, in company newsletters, or in briefing groups, of 'line of the month', 'best improved group', 'best operator', etc., with details of what the group or operator did to deserve the publicity spelled out, are commonplace.

Reward systems were always simple, with relatively few job classes and any differentials or bonuses being easily understood. Job classifications were, of course, deliberately kept to a minimum and job descriptions very broad to accommodate flexible working practices. Apart from 2 companies where complex job evaluation systems had been acquired from take-overs – and which were being systematically dismantled – the most job classes we came across, apart from hierarchical distinctions, was at a large company with five operator and five technician classes.

In 13 companies from which we were given the information, 7 claimed to pay in the upper quartile, 2 above average, and 4 average in relation to their local labour markets. Eight companies provided us with wage rates, and in these, basic operators earned between £126 and £202 per week, excluding overtime and bonuses. The average was £163. We should finally add that, despite the comments we made on redundancies and appraisals above, employees in Japanese transplants in Wales generally have enjoyed a relative stability of employment. For the past decade stable employment in Wales has not been easy to come by, and may be considered an additional welcome benefit.

Communications

All the companies we visited presented employees with a set of company rules, sometimes incorporated into an employee handbook. These explicitly lay down company policies on working hours, holidays, attendance and time-keeping, etc., together with procedures for breaches of discipline. The strictness with which rules are enforced is impressed on new recruits at induction sessions, and those with supervisory responsibilities, from team leader up, are expected to understand the rules and enforce them. The constant generation and communication of production, quality, efficiency, etc., information (discussed in detail in Chapter 4) is another means by which discipline is maintained, and systems of

Company newsletter	10
Daily team briefings	13
Weekly team briefings	4
Small group activities	14
Suggestion schemes	3

Table 5.5: *Formal communication mechanisms in Japanese companies in Wales (N = 23)*
Source: Author's Survey, 1992

'visible management' create a situation in which important information is communicated in a systematic manner. It is in these senses in which Japanese transplant management might be considered 'strict' or 'autocratic'.

At the same time, the style is very much one of 'talking problems through' and good face to face communications and interpersonal skills are typically one of the primary criteria for promotion or selection into team leader or supervisory positions. Three unjustified absences in a three month period might result in disciplinary action; the first absence will result in a counselling session where 'we ask them: have you got a problem at home? Is there anything we should know about?' The incidence of some of the more popularly known formal communication mechanisms are indicated in Table 5.5.

Most of the larger companies produce company newsletters which celebrate good company and team performances, communicate items such as investments, innovations and new products, and provide details of company-related social activities. As well as disseminating information, the newsletter is, of course, an attempt to make members feel a sense of belonging to the organization. Team briefings, on the other hand, often held for a few minutes at shift start, are primarily concerned with communicating the status of production, the efficiency and quality targets for the day, and any problems which are foreseen. As well as the daily briefing of teams, some companies have briefing systems which include meetings at various levels and times within the organization, serving to ensure everyone is in possession of the same accurate and timely information, and helping to prevent the spread of misinformation and ill-informed gossip.

Pension scheme	17
Medical insurance	19
Payment method	19
Working hours	21
Car park	19
Toilets	22
Canteen	22
All above single status	9

Table 5.6: *Single status facilities in Japanese companies in Wales (N = 22)*
Source: Authors' Survey, 1992.

Open communications are clearly facilitated by single status terms, conditions and facilities. These were widely in evidence, as shown in Table 5.6.

Company uniforms were compulsory in all but one case, where they were currently under consideration, although there were noticeable differences in the strictness with which the rule was applied. In a handful of cases companies had started up with company songs and pre-shift exercises, but in no case were these still practised.

Working patterns

Working hours ranged between 37 and 40, 39 being most common, with between one and four hours overtime per week (for operators, not managers who often worked long overtime hours unpaid) being typical. In many cases, overtime hours were artificially low due to the recession which was biting hard in early 1992 when the data was collected. In the majority of cases most employees worked only on day shifts, though two- and three-shift working was common for a minority of workers in some capital intensive sections of factories.

Many of the companies had to cope with seasonal variations in demand for their products. Carrying surplus labour or building to stock are, of course, anathema to Japanese-style production and work organization – instead the following means were used, in one case home workers were used to help out in high demand periods; in 7 cases companies could manage by significantly increasing overtime hours (up to 19 hours per week for a three-month period in the most extreme case); and in 9 cases temporary workers were used in addition to overtime in busy periods. Peaks and troughs were to be met in 3 companies through the introduction of annualized hours working during 1992. Managers' working hours were discussed in the previous chapter.

Personnel management in Japanese transplants in Wales shares some features in common with personnel practices in Japan – careful selection and the use of personal appraisals being two examples. Lifetime employment and extensive company welfare benefits, on the other hand, are examples of practices not introduced on to Welsh soil; nor should we expect them to be when the social environment is so different. What is important to Japanese transplants is that they utilize flexible, efficient labour, capable of working in teams and accepting strict discipline, and the personnel practices which are employed go a long way towards explaining an apparently high degree of success with Japanese-style production.

Six
Industrial Relations

For a Japanese-style production system with its tight staffing, flexible labour deployment and strict discipline, to work effectively, it is clear that *managerial prerogatives* are a prerequisite: union involvement in decisions on task allocation, for instance, would be time consuming and could result in inefficiencies as considerations other than the task at hand came into play. Another prerequisite is *stability of industrial relations*: with inventories, work-in-progress and stocks of finished goods held to a minimum, any stoppage will have immediate and pervasive consequences.[1] A stoppage even by one section of a factory where between-process stocks are strictly controlled can mean the whole factory grinding to a halt within hours.

In Japan, as is well documented, unions are enterprise based and largely incorporated; industrial disputes are relatively rare and the prerogatives of managers in most companies virtually complete.[2] Strong management prerogatives and stable industrial relations in Japan are not, as is frequently assumed, a simple reflection of Japanese culture, but the outcome of a complex history which saw militant and Communist-led trade unions ruthlessly repressed by the state and employers, with the blessing of the USA in the immediate post-war period. The modern form of incorporated enterprise unions is a relatively recent phenomenon.[3] None the less, such a form is well established already, Japanese employers appear happy with it, and Japanese companies have come to Wales and the UK looking for a similar degree of stability and freedom to manage. Not surprisingly, how Japanese companies would cope with British trade unions was to become a subject to fascinate industrial sociologists and journalists alike.

The immediate answer appears, of course, to be 'remarkably well', so well, in fact, that non-Japanese companies have sometimes more or less copied the collective agreements signed between Japanese companies and British unions. How well the unions have handled Japanese inward investment, on the other hand, is a subject of heated and highly emotive debate among British, and particularly Welsh, trade unionists. In this chapter we will provide a brief history of trade union responses to Japanese investment in Wales, then examine the characteristics of industrial relations in Japanese transplants in Wales in some detail.

The early arrivers: 1972–79

Even recent history is easily forgotten, and it is difficult to recall, and when we do recall, to believe, that this was a period when even fewer than one million unemployed was a national outrage, when a strike could bring down a government, and when unions were concerned not with membership, which was taken for granted, but with organization. Wales was a land of steel and coal, and it was the representatives of workers in these industries who commanded the headlines. Few people predicted, and even fewer acted upon, the dramatic transformation of Wales's political economy during the next decade (even though the transformation was, arguably, well under way). Nor was it conceived that the early Japanese investments in Wales were to be only the first among many, and that Japanese-generated employment was to become so important. This context may help explain why, despite trade union power, the early arrivers generated relatively little public controversy over their industrial relations arrangements.

In 1972 Takiron established the first Japanese company in Wales, and at first refused to recognize a union. USDAW requested, but was refused, recognition in 1973, but the TGWU, which had also been recruiting members within the plant, managed to secure a deal in 1976.[4] The second Japanese investor, Sony in 1973, was also the first to recognize a union: a deal was struck with the AEU even before the factory commenced operations. Sony's Director of European Operations was quoted as saying:

> We told them that we were only willing to negotiate through our designated trades union . . . we assured them that they could belong to any union of their choice, but if that particular union was not the designated trades union, it would have to negotiate with the Company's trade union . . . we have not experienced problems.[5]

Already, then, it appeared that the single union arrangement which Japanese companies enjoyed in Japan was the preferred option in Wales too, and this was confirmed in 1976 and again in 1978 when Panasonic and then Sekisui recognized the GMB and AEU respectively. A high degree of flexibility of labour deployment was enshrined in the Panasonic and Sony deals,[6] and of course the fact of single-union recognition is itself desirable by companies wishing to deploy flexible work practices. As Reitsperger has commented:

> Multi-union representation, and a resultant difficulty in flexibility and labour utilization, problems of demarcation and the complexity of multi-union bargaining are deeply worrying and seen by Japanese management as impediments to productive performance improvements.[7]

Although the term was not in vogue in the 1970s, 'beauty parades' were used by Japanese companies to come to a decision on which union would best fit their needs before employees were recruited. However, it was not until the 1980s that the 'beauty contest' syndrome became highly controversial. TGWU North Eastern Region Secretary, Joe Mills, was quoted as saying:

> Because of high unemployment and in desperation to cooperate with inward investment some unions are ignoring their traditional role . . . they are standing back and allowing companies to choose which union they want, similar to choosing washing powder from a supermarket.[8]

And Ken Gill, MSF General Secretary, said: 'These actions represent a desperate attempt to redefine trade unionism as a management service. *The employers – not the employees* – will choose the union.'[9]

The 'beauty parades' of the 1970s were organized by the Wales TUC which acted as a 'referral agency . . . for advice on achieving good industrial relations in newly establishing companies'.[10] The

Wales TUC cooperated with the WDA, ACAS, local authorities and other government and quasi-government organizations in facilitating the orderly establishment of trade unions and were seen by many as being instrumental in attracting inward investment. The Wales TUC was helping maintain an 'accord' between unions such that

> where a membership agreement has been reached prior to the company taking on staff, and where all relevant unions have been afforded an opportunity to put their case for recognition, those unions which have not been successful in securing an agreement have withdrawn their interest and have not sought to undermine the position of the successful union or unions.[11]

Such a policy has been justified on the grounds that the accord helped avoid inter-union disputes which could be damaging to the union movement as well as companies. Further

> It has resulted in the trade union movement maintaining a significant membership penetration in Wales and in the newer industries and this is in marked contrast to the membership 'wastelands' which have emerged in other parts of the UK.[12]

An additional reason why Japanese investors in Wales were, on the whole, welcomed by the Welsh union movement was provided by Wales TUC General Secretary, David Jenkins:

> The advantage of the Japanese is that they are more ready to accede at the outset the concept of unions. They are used to company unions in Japan, and may not trust them here, but they are used to the idea. American management, for instance, is much more opposed in principle.[13]

In a glossy publication published in 1986 and targeted at inward investors, Jenkins wrote:

> I would ask you to consider myself and my trade union colleagues as potential allies should you be considering investment in Wales, a country within the UK where industrial relations are making a positive contribution towards securing economic success.[14]

However, by then things were going seriously wrong. The Wales TUC was losing its role as adviser and referral agency to Japanese companies,[15] and inter-union disputes were beginning to break out.

The 1980s

The emergence of controversy surrounding single union deals in the 1980s related to a number of factors: the Wales TUC largely lost its role as referral agency; companies began going direct to unions and arguably, therefore, inviting inter-union squabbling; the nature of the agreements changed, particularly with the inclusion of no-strike clauses; and some companies moved towards recognition *after*, rather than in advance of, start-up. All this was in the context of a period when mass unemployment became a fact of life, and trade unions faced a crisis of membership. In Wales the trade union strongholds of coal and steel were decimated: coal was virtually wiped out; in steel, employment was slashed from 58,000 in the mid-1970s to around 16,000 in 1992.[16] Suddenly, membership recruitment was at the top of the union movement's agenda.[17]

The first blood to be spilled in Wales – at least publicly – was in 1984 when Hitachi, having taken sole ownership of the television plant in Hirwaun, signed a single union deal with the EETPU. The long-established factory had previously been wholly owned by GEC, and operated as a loss-making GEC–Hitachi joint venture between 1979 and 1984. Seeking a radical transformation of production and working practices, Hitachi gave its employees a document entitled *A New Future At Hirwaun*, spelling out a new set of working conditions and a commitment to the establishment of single status terms and facilities. It was not so much the new conditions which sparked the upset, however, but the fact that five long-established trade unions – the AEU, UCAAT, ASTMS, APEX and TASS – were suddenly excluded from bargaining. According to Tony Pegge, Hitachi's Personnel Executive through the changes:

> It is a fundamental principle of Hitachi, like most Japanese companies, that they do business with a single union. Hitachi employs more than a quarter of a million people throughout the world and in all of its businesses it does business with single unions . . . That was one fundamental change that they wanted to make, which we said to them was possible.[18]

On the 20 April 1984 a letter was sent to the six unions informing them that only the EETPU, because it had the majority membership, would be recognized. Then on the 27 April employees were told they would receive a 7 per cent pay rise across the board - the first rise since 1981. The workforce were expecting redundancies associated with rationalization and automation, and on the 11 May 500 were announced. Then during May and June the *New Future* document was negotiated - its fundamental principles remaining intact - with the EETPU.[19]

Not surprisingly, the unions excluded from bargaining at Hitachi took the case to the TUC on the grounds that the Bridlington agreement had been broken. However, according to Pegge the workers themselves

> believed that now here was the Japanese company which was going to give them a new status and conditions like the ones they had started to hear about at other Japanese companies in the UK who were giving, generally speaking, jobs for life . . . the people inside our factory weren't really interested in what they saw as a political matter to do with national officers of the trade unions . . . the members of AUEW [the largest of the excluded unions] told their national officer to go away, saying they did not want to go out on strike, which was the kind of thing that had been threatened. They said they did not want to upset Hitachi.[20]

The Hitachi agreement was the first of many single union agreements to be signed between the EETPU and Japanese companies in Wales. In April 1985 the TUC rebuked the EETPU for not approaching Hitachi in tandem with other unions, and for signing the agreement before the TUC had resolved the inter-union dispute.[21] But the agreement stood, and a rift was opened between the EETPU and other unions in Wales which was to become a gulf in the near future.

Upset amongst trade unionists was not wholly confined to the manner in which the Hitachi deal had been arrived at, but also its content. The deal was remarkably similar to the pioneering agreement signed between Toshiba and the EETPU in Plymouth in 1981, with provision for complete flexibility, a Company Members' Board serving as the first line in collective bargaining, and most controversially, what the EETPU euphemistically called a 'continuity of production' agreement, i.e. a no-strike clause (the full implications of these provisions are explored later). According to Pegge, Hitachi wanted 'a business relationship' with a single union with procedures that would 'make industrial action unnecessary'.[22] They actually got an agreement which ruled out official strikes as an option in the unions' arsenal of negotiating weapons.

The Hitachi–EETPU agreement was the one which sparked inter-union hostility in Wales. But it is interesting to note that this was not the first no-strike deal with a Japanese company in the principality. In fact, in 1982 the GMB had already signed such a deal with Aiwa following a beauty parade. In this agreement, Stage IV of the procedure for the avoidance of disputes reads:

> In the event of a 'failure to agree' the issue will be referred by mutual agreement between the Union and the Company to the Advisory, Conciliation and Arbitration Service for conciliation in the first instance. Subsequently, if appropriate, the issue will be referred by joint agreement for arbitration. In the latter case both parties accept that the decision is final and binding.[23]

The GMB did not break the terms of the Bridlington agreement, and had acted within the spirit of the accord between unions overseen by the Wales TUC. None the less, in retrospect it is remarkable that the GMB managed to keep its head down.

Between 1985 and 1988 the six single union agreements which had been signed between unions and Japanese companies in Wales were followed by a further ten. The EETPU, under its energetic Welsh leader Wyn Bevan, came out of the inter-union dispute over the Hitachi deal with a determination to gain more membership and with an almost arrogant confidence in the political and moral rightness of its methods and agreements. Eight of the ten agreements went to the EETPU, the other two to the GMB: the EETPU had come from nowhere to being the Japanese companies' favourite within the space of a few years, and was now actively and independently approaching Japanese companies well before the start-up of operations. However, it was at those companies which recruited staff and commenced production in advance of unionization that recognition disputes reached their height, in particular at Yuasa and Orion where the TGWU accused the EETPU of membership poaching and approaching the companies behind the back of other unions. Both these cases were referred to the TUC, which ordered a suspension of the deals pending investigation. Bevan later re-signed the agreement with Yuasa, and the Orion agreement eventually stood, but at the cost of the EETPU being expelled from the TUC.

George Wright, Wales TGWU leader, was the most outspoken against the developments in the mid-1980s. At the Wales TUC conference in 1987 he said Japanese companies were employing 'samurai management' methods and expecting to operate in a 'coolie economy'. Japanese firms coming to Wales were bringing 'unwanted labour practices', setting 'impossible conditions', and demanding 'total subservience and the freedom to manage'. He went on: 'Enough is enough. They had better change their ways. If you operate in this country you live by our standards and observe the rights of democratic people.'[24]

Interestingly, a year later, the then Welsh Secretary of State, Peter Walker, whilst giving a speech at the opening of the new Hitachi microwave oven plant, congratulated the EETPU on its deals.[25] Wright and Walker presumably had different conceptions of democracy in mind.

The Orion deal was signed at a time when the TGWU claimed it had nearly 80 per cent support among the workers in its application for recognition. The EETPU defended its refusal to relinquish the deal, despite a TUC ruling against them on the grounds that management did not wish to deal with the TGWU and so the alternative would be no union recognition at all.[26] The agreement became one of two test cases (the other being a similar agreement with Christian Salvesen, a Cheshire-based distribution company) which led to expulsion from the TUC for the EETPU on the 5 September 1988. On the day of expulsion the GMB's national leader John Edmonds led a bitter attack on the EETPU's recent record:

> People want to join unions because they want to, not because their boss delivers them in bulk supply, as part of some shabby sweetheart deal. We are not here to do a favour for Lord Hanson or pout prettily at Rupert Murdoch.[27]

In fact, during the same year the GMB *had* 'done a favour' for two Japanese companies in South Wales when it signed no-strike agreements following beauty contests with Electronic Harnesses and Star Micronics. But somehow the union, amidst the furore over the EETPU's flagrant disregard of TUC's instructions, again managed to avoid the headlines.

Since 1988 the EETPU has continued to sign no-strike deals, and its Welsh leader, Wyn Bevan, has commented that

> its independence outside the TUC has not inhibited in any way its ability to conclude agreements with inward-investment companies. Our proven success record continues because we are able to demonstrate conclusively to employers that our continuity of production arrangements really does work.[28]

Two of these deals in Wales have been with Japanese companies – at Matsushita's new magnetron plant (1990) and at Tsuda (1991). The AEU secured a deal at Meiki, and in three cases Japanese companies 'acquired' trade unions – at Zeon, Calsonic and the Lucas–Sumitomo joint venture. Most intriguing, perhaps, has been two single union agreements recently signed by the TGWU – at Hoya in 1989 (Hoya had resisted unionization since it set up in 1980) and at the Gooding–Sanken joint venture in 1990. The latter agreement has a disputes procedure which ends in binding pendulum arbitration.

After all the fighting of the 1980s, in recent years inter-union conflict has declined. Japanese companies have hence continued to establish deals with single unions with the special provisions which help maintain industrial peace and ensure managerial prerogatives, but without the controversy and special media attention. The big four unions, whether with enthusiasm as in the case of the EETPU, or with reservations and after soul searching, as we must presume has been the case with the TGWU and perhaps the GMB, have all now established such agreements. It seems unlikely then, that for the foreseeable future the established pattern of industrial relations in Japanese companies in Wales will change. The question we turn to now is the implications of the new style agreements for management and employees in Japanese transplants.

Trade union recognition: facts and figures

Across the whole of Britain Japanese companies have consistently established industrial relations systems with either no union or a

EETPU	11
GMB	3
GMB and APEX	1
AEU	3
AEU, APEX and MSF	1
AEU, TGWU, EETPU and MSF	1
TGWU	2
None	2

Table 6.1: *Trade union recognition in Japanese companies in Wales (N = 24)*
Source: Authors' Survey, 1992.

single union: generally, no union in new towns and semi-rural locations (such as many Japanese companies in Scotland, Telford and Milton Keynes), and a single union in locations with a strong industrial and trade union tradition. Sites chosen by Japanese companies in both North and South Wales, of course, fit the latter category. Of the 24 companies in which we documented industrial-relations practices in 1992, 22 had recognized trade unions. The unions recognized are indicated in Table 6.1. Of the three exceptional companies which recognize more than one union, one has virtually identical agreements with the GMB and its white-collar section APEX, and in the other two cases the companies recently acquired more than one trade union on brownfield sites.

Membership densities varied between 30 per cent and 100 per cent, with no significant differences among the unions. Average membership density across 18 companies which provided us with the figures was 63 per cent, and even higher at 69 per cent when calculating on the basis of total employees in all companies: these figures compare favourably with the averages both for Japanese companies in the rest of Britain, and for non-Japanese manufacturing companies in Britain.[29] High membership levels are explained in part by the facts that most Japanese companies implicitly or explicitly encourage union membership during inductions, and provide check-off facilities so that members cannot simply allow their membership to lapse, but have to make a conscious decision and effort not to pay their dues: a manager at one company used exactly such reasoning to explain why, despite apathy towards the trade union by workers, membership was virtually 100 per cent.

Shop steward representation per employee varied between 1 per 191 and 1 per 15 employees. (One very small manufacturer at the time had no shop stewards, but hoped to correct the situation shortly.) Average representation was 1 shop steward per 76 employees, and 1 shop steward per 49 union members. Calculated on the basis of total eligible employees in all companies (assuming 85 per cent eligibility) the figures were 1 per 85 and 1 per 59, respectively.

Eighteen companies provided us with details of their collective agreements, so that we could analyse the incidence of key features which have been subject to controversy. Table 6.2 gives a summary, and we will organize our discussion of industrial relations in Japanese transplants around these features.

Flexibility clause	15
Communication clause	8
CoAB or equivalent for collective bargaining	11
Binding arbitration	14
Pendulum arbitration	6
Company commitment to training clause	10

Table 6.2: *Features of collective agreements in Japanese companies in Wales (N = 18)*
Source: Authors' Survey, 1992.

Flexibility

As will be clear by now, a flexible deployment of labour is a prerequisite for a Japanese-style manufacturing system to operate efficiently and effectively. In eliminating the possibility of inter-union demarcation disputes, a single-union arrangement removes one potential barrier to flexible working. Japanese companies in Wales (and elsewhere in Britain) have, however, gone one step further: in 15 of the 18 collective agreements we have studied, a flexibility clause unambiguously establishes management's right to deploy labour as it sees fit. An agreement signed by the EETPU reads:

> Both the company and the union recognize and support that full flexibility of jobs and duties within the company are necessary and will

> continue in order to enhance the future job security of all company employees. It is clearly understood that all employees will perform whatever job or duties are within their capability in order to maintain and develop the operating efficiency and commercial success of the company.

A clause in an agreement signed by the GMB is equally unambiguous:

> The company and the union jointly agree that it is a further condition of employment that each employee accepts the direction of the company's management to perform any kind or type of work within the employee's known abilities. Refusal to accept such direction may be regarded as gross industrial misconduct and could render an employee liable to disciplinary action.

And the same is true in an agreement signed by the TGWU:

> Employees will agree to the complete flexibility of jobs and duties within and between the company's functions and departments. The main principle of flexibility is, when necessary, to meet the needs of the company. All employees will perform whatever jobs or duties are within their degree of skill, experience and capabilities having due regard to safety.

We did come across one company which consulted with shop stewards before moving workers between factories on the same site, but flexible labour deployment was a fact of life at all the Japanese companies visited, a practice which has proved notoriously difficult to establish in many British companies.[30] This is partly because agreeing to complete managerial prerogatives over labour deployment not only improves labour utilization, but signs away a potential bargaining counter and takes from the role of shop steward in mediating the relationship between supervisor and worker. An advantage of the flexibility agreement claimed by some trade unionists, on the other hand, is the single-status terms and conditions which normally go with it, as detailed in the previous chapter. Also typically accompanying the flexibility clause is a statement that the company is committed to training employees. These features are part of the justification of the new deals, and the EETPU has claimed they contribute to the breakdown of the British system of 'industrial apartheid'. Wyn Bevan has commented:

> The single status element speaks for itself. It simply means that the only differential between staff is the rate of pay, thus dissolving the artificial barriers that in many instances are still prevalent in British Industry. . . . Inter-union demarcation lines are a thing of the past and flexibility depends on nothing more than receiving the necessary training to carry out the task required. By adopting this approach, it has been found that job satisfaction is increased and it has been recognized, at least by those who operate within the agreements, that the security of the workforce is inexorably linked to the success of the enterprise.[31]

Few would wish to argue – at least not publicly – with the desirability of removing status distinctions from the workplace. However, to the extent that workers, as a result, identify with the company, as Bevan suggests they do, it could be argued that the rationale for union representation may be undermined. This is an issue we shall return to later.

Communications

As we have seen in the previous two chapters, communications are taken seriously in Japanese companies in Wales: effectively they are, indeed, built into the system of production and management. Like flexibility, communications also have implications for trade unions: as popular wisdom has it, 'information is power', and as Nissan's Director of Personnel has declared, 'He who communicates is King'.[32] In an interview with one of the authors it was a trade union official, who ironically was responsible for overseeing more than one single union agreement in Wales, who summed up the effect:

> They want the opportunity for the management always to have a right to talk to the groups or to the workforce in totality by any methods. When I was a shop steward I'd call a strike if they did that. Traditionally British shop stewards don't allow it: one, they are afraid that the management will be able to convince members to do something that the shop stewards committee would be against, and two, they would say it in a different way than I would say it as a shop steward. If I wasn't happy with a deal then I certainly would portray it in a way which would be biased towards my thinking. The Japanese wouldn't allow that at all . . . They believe in taking people with them. What better way can you have of taking the workforce with you than for the workforce to suggest the changes that you want them to suggest anyway?

Here, then, is another way in which the traditional role of the British shop steward as mediator of the manager–worker nexus is undermined in Japanese transplants. And again, there are arguments in favour of extensive, direct communications which trade unionists may find difficulty in refuting. A common complaint against British managements has been the lack of communication of relevant information, so that the employee can neither understand his or her role in relation to others in the organization nor how the company is doing and what the future might hold. When an employer does provide such information and the management is neither aloof, distant or secretive, it is difficult for a union to argue that it has the sole right to broadcast. Just to make sure, some of the single union agreements have specific communications clauses – 8 out of the 18 we have studied. For instance:

> T&GWU accepts that the company reserves the right to address its employees singularly or in groups during working hours upon whatever matter the company deems appropriate and accepts that each individual employee retains the right of access to the company.

And, in a GMB agreement: 'The union accepts that the company will brief employees singly or in groups during their stay on company premises.'

It is difficult to imagine a Japanese company on a greenfield site in Wales finding it necessary to appeal to such a clause, but its existence in some cases demonstrates the importance attached to communication by Japanese manufacturers. It preempts the possibility – at least within the terms of the agreement – of the union taking advantage of a powerful source of influence at some point in the future.

Consultation

In terms of industrial relations, consultation is, of course, one of the key aspects of communication, and it is not surprising that formal consultation mechanisms are in place *and* taken seriously in most Japanese companies. We came across only two exceptions: both of these are small organizations employing fewer than 40 people where informal consultation was considered adequate.

Consultation is the area in which the agreements signed by the EETPU stand out from the rest, at least in Wales: in the case of EETPU agreements the consultative forum considers and makes recommendations on issues traditionally the preserve of collective bargaining between company and union; in the other agreements bargaining is a separate event.[33] The first agreement in Britain enshrining such a form of consultation was that between Toshiba and the EETPU in Plymouth, where it is stated that:

> The function of the [union] representative will be to represent union members on those issues which cannot be resolved through the Company Advisory Board and to represent individual members of the trade union in cases of individual grievances, discipline or other related matters.[34]

Within Wales it was Hitachi who first embraced such an institution, giving it the title 'company members' board'. Pegge has described it as 'the main organ of consultation activity and change implementation',[35] and it is worth elaborating on its functioning.

When Hitachi took sole control of the Hirwaun plant in 1984, the new agreement required new elections for representatives in 20 newly defined constituencies (there had been 58 shop stewards prior to the new deal). Those representatives elected who are EETPU members are called shop stewards, but membership of the EETPU, or any other union, is not a condition of representation. The 20 constituencies are grouped together to produce 8 company members' board (CMB) constituencies, and second elections produce 8 company members' board representatives. The EETPU convener and deputy convener have CMB positions automatically, and the remaining 7 (total 17) seats are taken up by a team leaders' representative, a middle management representative, a senior management representative, and 4 management appointments. The CMB meets monthly to discuss a range of information provided by the company on topics such as business plans, efficiency and performance, manpower plans, and the working environment – hence it acts as a traditional consultative committee. 'More significantly', according to Pegge, it is 'the first stage in the company's collective issue resolution procedure.'[36] This involves provision by the company to representatives a range of pertinent information such as pay and conditions at competitor companies and in local labour markets, company accounts, profitability, and background UK economic figures, such as RPI and GNP history and forecasts. The CMB then strives to produce a consensus view and make a consensus recommendation, which is put to the shop stewards/ representatives committee and to the managing director. If one or both sides reject the recommendation, negotiation between the EETPU and the company's management goes ahead.

Whilst EETPU agreements sometimes differ in the specifics of constitution and procedure for consultation (for instance, in some cases only EETPU members sit on the board) the fundamentals are the same. The board is an institution for the dissemination and discussion of important company information. And it is the first line in collective bargaining. Some companies insist that representatives/shop stewards sign a form committing them to the board. At one company, for instance, the form reads:

> I accept that all grievances and disputes must be resolved within the agreed procedures. I recognize that the Company Advisory Committee is the first means of resolving all collective issues and I fully support and encourage the role of the Company Advisory Committee.

Herein lies a problem for the trade union: to the extent that the members' board (or company advisory board) is successful in achieving consensus recommendations acceptable to both company management and employees, the trade union is either marginalized (if it disagrees with the recommendations) or incorporated (if it fully supports the board and its recommendation).[37] In most companies, most of the recommendations of the board are accepted most of the time. The advantages of the successful functioning of such institutions claimed for trade union members, on the other hand, include the provision of information which might otherwise be kept secret, and the further breaking down of barriers between 'them and us'.[38] What is clear, is that the company members' board implies a change in the traditional role of trade union as adversary towards one of cooperation with the employer.

Continuity of Production

If the provisions for labour deployment, communications and consultation enshrined in single union agreements undermine the traditional sources of power and influence of the shop steward, the continuity of production provision strips away the ultimate sanction of the whole union – industrial action. In 14 out of the 18 agreements we studied, collective procedures ended in binding arbitration, and in 6 of these 14, the arbitrator is instructed to find on a pendulum basis. This means that in these 14 cases any industrial action could take place only outside the terms of the agreement, and whilst collective agreements are not legally enforceable,[39] it is highly unlikely that a trade union would dishonour an agreement in such a fundamental way. With this qualification, the term 'no-strike deal' is accurate.

Negotiating procedures as enshrined in the agreement tend to be lengthy, starting with the members' board (where one exists) and moving to the next stage if the board fails to come to a consensus or the company or union reject the recommendation. The next stages are typically negotiation between company and internal union representatives, then involvement of outside union officials will be sought. Sometimes provision for a secret ballot is made if there is failure to agree at this point. Referral to ACAS for conciliation is likely to come next, and finally (in 14 out of the 18 cases) ACAS is requested to appoint an arbitrator for a binding decision. The intent, which is often spelled out, is to resolve all disputes as early as possible in the procedure: the final stage of binding arbitration is considered a backstop. In the case of pendulum arbitration, the intention is to encourage both sides not to make outrageous and unjustifiable demands or offers as part of bargaining strategy, but to be 'realistic' from the beginning.

Trade unionists supportive of strike-free arrangements point out that strikes are costly to employees as well as employers, and that there are better means of settling disputes than a fight to the death. The EETPU has also pointed out that no-strike agreements with binding arbitration are often resisted by *employers* because 'they remove management's right to impose what settlement it likes'.[40] The critics, however, have been unconvinced. Ken Gill, then General Secretary of TASS, commented:

> The difference between a slave and a worker is the right to withdraw his labour. So while the pendulum arbitration agreement does not specifically forbid strikes, it obliges both sides to accept the arbitrator's verdict, thereby denying the worker the ultimate expression of rejection.[41]

During the late 1980s the TUC hotly debated, but failed to implement, a code of conduct on single union agreements which would forbid, or greatly restrict, member unions signing away the right to strike. George Wright, on the other hand, appealed to the Japanese government to urge Japanese companies not to seek strike-free arrangements. Wright said the first 10 or 11 Japanese companies to come to Wales had followed Wales TUC procedures in choosing and recognizing a union. Companies arriving in the mid-1980s were setting up without a union, then when unions such as the TGWU began recruiting and seeking recognition, they would turn to the EETPU for a no-strike deal.[42] Since then, new Japanese investors have not been troubled by inter-union recognition disputes, but they have continued to sign no-strike deals, and even the TGWU conceded the right to strike in one agreement: for all practical purposes, the critics of the strike-free element of the single union package have, at least for the time being, lost the argument.

We did not document a single case of a dispute going to arbitration in a Japanese company in Wales. Interestingly, there was one such case at Sanyo in Lowestoft, which has a pendulum arbitration agreement with the EETPU. Here, in December 1984 pendulum arbitration was avoided at the last moment when ACAS mediation was successful,[43] but in April 1988 an impasse in pay negotiations was reached with the EETPU asking for 8.5 per cent and Sanyo offering 6 per cent. The arbitrator awarded in favour of the EETPU.[44]

Of course, a no-strike agreement does not wholly rule out the possibility of industrial action, it only means that the union can neither instigate nor support such action. We documented industrial action in 8 Japanese companies in Wales. In three cases the disputes were national ones relating to working hours. One company which was not unionized at the time suffered two walkouts in the early 1980s – one over alleged 'mistreatment' of an employee by a supervisor, and the other in response to an alleged 'unfair dismissal'; both disputes were resolved within hours. Another company with a single-union deal without binding arbitration faced a stoppage during pay negotiations in 1981: the following day members accepted the same offer and managers attributed the disruption to the inexperience of shop stewards. In the sixth case, shop stewards led unofficial action, despite a no-disruption agreement, in the company's maintenance area in protest against the introduction of a system whereby a certain percentage of the wage bill would be allocated among individual workers according to appraisal results: the company quickly won the dispute. In the seventh case, a joint-venture company which had acquired a conventional agreement, faced a two week overtime ban during pay negotiations in 1991: the pay offer was eventually accepted as it stood. The eighth dispute we documented was at Hitachi. Three hundred workers staged a sit-in protest at the delay of company and union in settling a pay dispute: the protest came to an end on the same day.[45] Apart from the first three cases mentioned, where the company was unavoidably affected by a national dispute, in only two cases did a company with a continuity of production agreement face action, although industrial relations in Japanese companies in Wales overall have been so remarkably stable that it is impossible to draw any conclusions from this relating to the arguments for and against the no-strike clause.

Conclusions

The EETPU has actively sought and signed single-union agreements with all the features described above. Its justification is that the alternative may be no union representation at all, and more positively, that there are gains for members in terms of single-status terms, good communications, a company commitment to training, and a breaking down of the barriers between 'us and them'. Critics question whether the 'gains' are not, in fact, features of human resource management which would in any case be implemented by the Japanese, and whether companies might have been willing to pay more to their employees as a 'rent' against unionization by the likes of the TGWU or MSF. The trade union membership crisis, however, has forced most unions over the past decade to rethink or, in practice, to abandon their principles, and the strike-free agreement, complete with flexibility and communication clauses, has become the norm for inward investing companies. At the 1991 TUC conference, a motion was carried condemning the 'alien' industrial relations practices brought to Britain by the Japanese. But few unions will refuse to endorse such practices when they have the opportunity to sign an agreement which gives membership. As one union leader in Wales commented to one of the authors: 'A few years ago Nissan and Hitachi couldn't have happened. Now we're all in the shit. This is what leads trade unions to sign these sorts of agreement: the chase, the desperate need for membership.'

Out of the 1980s, led by Japanese investors and the EETPU, with a good deal of the drama played out on Welsh soil, has emerged a new form of industrial relations, one so popular amongst employers that agreements with the same essential features are being pursued in companies across the UK. This is a unitarist form of industrial relations where fundamental differences of interest between employer and employee are not admitted, where, in the words of one typical agreement:

> The management and the union have a common objective in ensuring the efficiency and prosperity of the company for the benefit of shareholders, all employees and customers.

SEVEN

Japan in Wales: Japanese Manufacturing and the Welsh Community

In Chapters 3 to 6 we have considered the impact of Japanese manufacturing investment on the local economy, work organization and industrial relations. The effects of local concentrations of Japanese investment on the region go further than this. In Chapter 3 it was shown that Japanese investors have created substantial employment in Wales. In some areas, i.e. Bridgend, Wrexham and Cardiff, individual Japanese enterprises are amongst the largest local employers. As such these companies have the accompanying potential to create both positive and negative social and economic externalities.

Japanese investors in Wales have been very conscious of the public perceptions of their activities, and have been equally anxious to be perceived as good corporate citizens. The Japanese companies in Wales have a number of skills both at the organizational and human level. These skills may possibly be brought to bear on local government, education, environment and society in Wales. In sum, the skills of Japanese enterprise can be applied to challenges in other sectors of Welsh society and life.

In this chapter there is firstly an assessment of the role of local Japanese enterprise as good corporate citizens. We will consider the impact of Japanese plants in the local community through an examination of the linkages that have been developed. The second section looks specifically at the experiences of Japanese personnel and their families in the Welsh community. This section examines what the Japanese in Wales perceive as the positive and negative consequences of the tour of duty in the region. There is also an assessment of the importance of the Welsh posting in career terms for the Japanese manager. The final section considers the growing social and cultural linkage between Wales and Japan, and the extent to which the presence of the Japanese investment in Wales has stimulated these linkages.

Japanese corporate involvement

The level and extent of Japanese company involvement in their local communities is in the majority of cases a function of both their size and time of establishment. The larger more established Japanese enterprises in consumer electronics often have local links which are too numerous to mention. As part of our survey of Japanese manufacturing investment in Wales, company managers were invited to comment upon the nature of their corporate links in the community. Table 7.1. shows instances where responding companies specifically noted community links.

Nearly three quarters of the Japanese firms have linkages with local schools. These ties are normally with secondary schools, but one company in South Wales was actively building linkages with local primary schools. The chief accountant at the firm mentioned that:

> We are now looking to extend help to local primary schools. We gave one school a big electronic circuit board which is a teaching aid (to teach

Schools (primary and secondary)	15
Higher education colleges (inc. universities)	12
Local authorities and trade associations	13
Chambers of commerce	8
Training and enterprise councils	12
Local charities	9
Local sporting linkages/sponsorship	14
Other community links	6
Few community links	3

Table 7.1: *Japanese corporate linkages in local communities (N = 21).*
Source: Authors' Survey, 1992
Note: Indicates where linkages were specifically mentioned.

> basic electronics). We wanted to pass it from school to school but they like it so much they won't let it go!

The nature of Japanese company linkages with secondary schools varied greatly. One personnel manager in a large Japanese firm in South Wales said in this respect:

> We provide materials, donate colour televisions, and provide old PCBs for school project work. We also participate in work experience programmes. Young people often come to work in the office . . . as many as six at a time. There is no formal process, it just occurs.

Another Japanese company had a Business in Schools programme and during 1991 noted that 40 pupils had undertaken work experience within their plant. Other forms of involvement included participation in education partnership trusts. Sony at Bridgend chairs the Ogwr Borough Young Enterprise scheme. Other firms are involved through tutoring in school business projects. Corporate governorships among managers in Japanese plants are widespread, as are instances of linkages with school career sections, and education steering committees. Overall Japanese company linkages with local education were fairly extensive and, importantly, they are growing.

Few Japanese companies in Wales have had any technically based associations with either colleges of higher education in Wales or universities. In part this is a function of the fact that many of the plants are of recent origin. However, this lack of linkage is also a function of the operational nature of Japanese plants in the Welsh economy. One of the reasons that locally based research and development is desired among subsidiaries is so that technically based linkages will evolve with local higher education institutions. Specific examples of Japanese involvement with local universities are few. Two Japanese firms mentioned that they have been aided by projects carried out in Welsh universities, or that they had sponsored projects. For example, one consumer electronics maker in North Wales was involved with the Electronic and Systems Engineering Department (ELSYM) at the University of Wales College of Cardiff in an automation based project, and Sony at Bridgend has provided ELSYM with some robots. In other cases students on MSc programmes in engineering at Cardiff have undertaken projects at Japanese companies such as Aiwa and Hitachi, covering topics such as stock control, and the design of microwave ovens.

Although the nature of technically based collaboration has been limited, Japanese enterprise in Wales has been fairly open to enquiries from academics within Wales into the nature of their operational practices. Firms such as Sony and Matsushita are bombarded at regular intervals with requests for information from both academics and students alike. In most instances Japanese firms have accommodated study-based visits, although in doing so a great deal of valuable staff time is used. Evidence for this is found in the many books and articles where firms such as Sony, and Matsushita are used as exemplars of inward investment, and best operational practices.

The main linkages occurring between Japanese firms and higher education establishments have normally been for recruitment and training purposes, or for the placement of engineering and business studies students who are studying on sandwich type degree schemes. It was shown in Chapter 4 that the majority of Japanese firms have a strong emphasis of workforce development and training. In this context personnel working for Japanese enterprise have used local colleges for professional training, i.e. courses leading to professional qualifications in personnel, management accounting, purchasing and technical functions. Beyond this the nature of collaboration remains limited.

A number of Japanese subsidiaries are either in the process of or have already developed links with local training and enterprise councils (TECs). The nature of involvement with the councils differs from case to case. In some instances involvement has been limited to just informal contacts, but in other cases managing directors of Japanese plants sit on local councils, or firms have received grants and are actively involved in TEC schemes. For example, two Japanese electronics firms in South Wales have encouraged employees to participate in TEC-based vocational training. Aiwa (Newport) has, with the aid of training consultants, developed a programme which allows trainees to gain a Level 2 City and Guilds qualification in Machining, Assembly and Processing Skills (MAPS). Ten supervisors within the firm have already been trained as work-based trainers to monitor individuals participating in the scheme. The qualification allows the employees of the firm to gain a nationally recognized qualification in the workplace where there was no provision previously. In addition Aiwa, as part of a £15,000 training programme financed by a Business Growth Training Award from Gwent TEC, have established a Management Improvement Programme. At Gooding Sanken (Aberdare) 30 employees are involved in a MAPS scheme, with 20 additional employees waiting to follow.

Japanese companies in Wales have all had dealings with local councils, development agencies and trade associations during their initial feasibility work and settling in period within Wales. Local and county councils (together with the WDA) have aided firms with finding factories, housing provision or making various administrative arrangements. This assistance has been very much appreciated, especially among those Japanese investors who were very much the pioneers of Japanese inward investment in Wales. The extent to which formal links has been maintained between local councils varies. Two Japanese companies specifically noted the maintenance of strong links. In both cases the subsidiaries were key employers in their respective areas. The Welsh managing director of one of these firms stated that:

> We have . . . close links with the local authorities as part of the regeneration of the Cynon Valley. (Two managers) are on the business partnership team in Cynon Valley. As a company our principle is to try and integrate, and put something back in . . . not just creation of employment.

A Japanese company in North Wales (the largest local employer), maintained close links with the local council through a series of quarterly meetings between top plant management and council officials, as well as through sponsorship of council events and festivals.

In many instances the local success of Japanese manufacturers has been used by local councils and the Welsh Development Agency to promote both specific areas and Wales generally as a location for further inward investment. Eight Japanese manufacturers mentioned linkages with local chambers of commerce. The bulk of the more established subsidiaries are members of the Wales CBI, and some of the largest employers have seats on the Wales Council of this body. And as described in Chapter 6, other subsidiaries noted that the Wales TUC had aided them in the signing of collective agreements with their workforces.

One of the most important Japanese corporate interfaces with the community is through sports and social links. The larger Japanese manufacturers in Wales have active sports and social clubs providing outings for employees, charity events and organized sports. Few companies actually provide extensive facilities for sport, although one company in North Wales was an exception. The local senior general manager mentioned that:

> The company has a sports and social committee of which I am the Treasurer. Membership costs £1 per month. It runs football, netball, squash, cricket and softball (for the Japanese). The company funds 50 per cent of the expenditure. They have provided a football pitch and changing rooms. The Japanese like to see people involved on the sporting side.

Some Japanese firms provide newsletters for their staff which give ample evidence of extensive sports and social commitments outside the plant. A local manager in another Japanese plant mentioned:

> Various societies within the firm cater for sports. Six-a-side matches are organised internally and externally. They have organised and sponsored a number of events, cultural and sporting in the locality. They also run competitions between shifts. We sponsor some junior teams locally, and second division rugby teams, and a local football team.

In the majority of cases sports and social linkages (including charity support) were established in the locality immediately around plants, although two Japanese companies in North Wales sponsor Barclay's English First Division football teams.

Japanese employees are keen to take advantage of local golfing facilities which are far cheaper and more spacious than similar facilities in Japan. Some companies have taken out corporate membership of select local clubs. One local manager commented on the social importance of golf to Japanese personnel:

> All the Japanese have joined the golf clubs . . . for the Japanese golf is a business meeting as well as relaxation. It does break down barriers – on the golf course you are more of an equal. The Japanese have to

> lobby people to get consensus as part of their local decision making, so out of work activities are crucial.

Japanese companies in Wales also have other linkages within their local communities. One Japanese company in Wrexham was supporting a Japanese collection in the local library. Several firms have open days where local communities are invited to come and see what is actually done in the plants. One Japanese company in North Wales has actively joined forces with local residents to fight a British Coal open cast development. The company is advising local residents and providing financial aid for legal costs.

In summary, a number of Japanese manufacturers in Wales desire to become key players not only in the local economy but also in the local community. There are a growing number of linkages between Japanese manufacturing companies and their local communities as the subsidiaries seek over time to become responsible corporate citizens.

Japanese personnel in Wales

Estimates as to the total number of Japanese expatriate personnel in Wales at any one time vary greatly. This is partly to be expected as numbers fluctuate. Some personnel are only on very brief secondments to aid technical or product change or plant start ups. Other managers are based locally from anywhere from three to ten years. Japanese companies have where possible delegated managerial and technical positions to local staff as it is expensive to retain Japanese personnel in Wales. However, only one Japanese manufacturing plant in Wales has no Japanese expatriate staff on the plant site, with the largest plant having 45 Japanese personnel. In total there are over 200 Japanese personnel working in the manufacturing subsidiaries alone. In total, when families, and other Japanese nationals in Wales are included, the Japanese population in Wales may top 1,300, making this one of the largest Japanese communities in the UK.

For many Japanese personnel Wales is the first foreign posting. In this section we show how Japanese personnel have adjusted to life in Wales. Initially there is an examination of the positive and negative points of the posting from the point of view of Japanese personnel. The concluding section seeks to assess the extent to which a posting in Wales benefits the career of the Japanese manager. The material in this section is based around interviews with a total of 17 Japanese managers, including 8 managing directors, which were carried out as part of our research in 1992.

Positive and negative experiences

The factors that Japanese managers had noted as positive are shown in Table 7.2. The warm general welcome received in Wales has been very much appreciated by the Japanese. There was every indication that this had been important to some of those who had been posted in other areas of the world previously. Several managers said that Japanese personnel did not get such a welcome in other areas of the world, possibly implying regions within the Pacific Rim. In addition to this 5 managers specifically pointed out that they thought that Wales was a safe place to live. The ease of integration into local communities was appreciated. One Japanese financial director commented: 'It is probably worse for UK people going out to Japan than vice versa. We settle well in the UK.'

A company in North Wales had encouraged its personnel to disperse within the locality. The managing director commented 'there are no Japanese ghettoes – this was a policy decision and it is rare to find two in the same local community'. The same managing director noted that his Japanese staff were not asking him for permission to go home! Similar sentiments were expressed by the managing director of a Japanese electronics firm in South Wales: 'I've been here for almost six years . . . since start up, so my

Warm welcome in Wales	6
General working environment	9
Reduced commuting times	2
Travelling/holiday opportunities	4
Sporting opportunities	7
Safe living environment	5
Career development	9
Availability of fish	1

Table 7.2: *Positive factors associated with a Welsh posting (N = 17)*
Source: Authors' Survey, 1992.

term is almost finishing. Going back to Japan will be difficult for me. I prefer to stay here longer.'

In South Wales, however, one Japanese manager felt that Japanese ghettoes were being formed with resultant problems for Japanese wives:

> There is a slight problem because now there are around 50 Japanese families, and they tend to establish Japanese communities. Japanese wives especially tend to stick together, and it might be better if they integrated more with the wider community. But they find it very comfortable to live here.

In a similar vein another Japanese managing director in South Wales said that: 'They [Japanese wives] get together quite often . . . so the wives don't need to speak English, which is not good for them.'

The Welsh posting seems to be a lonelier experience for Japanese wives than their husbands. Japanese executives have the company organization to aid their adaptation to the local way of life. Japanese wives in the region cannot often get working permits, and are expected in many cases to look after the home. A strong network does exist between the wives of Japanese managers stationed in Wales, and this has mitigated some of the problems of coming to a new area. Learning the language remains a significant hurdle in their achieving fuller integration into local communities.

In one case in a smaller Japanese company in North Wales, local executives had strongly advised their two Japanese managers to live in a village where there were no other Japanese to encourage some integration. One Japanese manager had taken this advice, and his wife who had initially been fearful of coming to Wales, had integrated into the local community extremely well.

Japanese managers have appreciated the rural scenery and the slower pace of life more generally in Wales. One Japanese managing director mentioned:

> Compared to Japan, commuting is easier. In Japan I live near Tokyo and commuting takes a long time on a crowded train. Here its a five minute drive. This place is less crowded and more comfortable. Its easy to go the theatre, and there are many local places to visit.

However, easier commuting had created one problem for this manager in particular:

> Easy commuting means more work and lack of exercise. I used to get exercise walking between stations and travelling standing up on crowded trains. Now my arm and leg power has dropped!

Another manager, whilst enjoying opportunities for sightseeing and sports in Wales, noted ruefully: 'but no hot springs, no bar hopping, no ladies!'

Some of the managers were at pains to point out that they still worked those same long hours as in Japan. One manager in South Wales commented, 'Typically I work 8.00 am to 10.30 pm. I worked 3,300 hours in 1991. From this year I hope it will be less hours', and a managing director in North Wales mentioned, 'Japanese managers working hours are similar to those in Japan – 8 am to 7 or 8 pm each week day and some Saturday mornings.' In spite of this other managers, whilst working similar hours, were taking advantage of travelling and holidaying opportunities available whilst on a Welsh posting. A managing director in a Japanese electronics company in South Wales commented:

> Travelling on holidays is far easier. In Japan we don't have enough holidays. Here I can have two weeks in the summer and ten days at Christmas. Working hours are similar here to Japan. Monday to Thursday we work 13 hours, and less on Friday. When we started I worked weekends as well but not now . . . in the summer the Japanese rush out to the golf course.

With respect to travelling and sightseeing Welsh postings have made European holiday destinations more accessible for Japanese managers in both financial and physical terms.

The main difficulties associated with the Welsh posting by Japanese managers are summarized in Table 7.3.

By far the most common problem is the education of children. The comments about education difficulties were not always a criticism of the local system. As one Japanese managing director pointed out: 'There is nothing wrong with the education system here provided Japanese children stay in it, and are not shifted back to Japan.' This particular manager regretfully noted that his son

Education of children	12
Language problems	6
Difficulty integrating wives into local communities	4
Missing family and friends	2
Missing Japanese food	2
No problems noted	2
Other	6

Table 7.3: *Negative factors associated with a Welsh posting (N = 17).*
Source: Authors' Survey, 1992.

was already a poor speaker of Japanese. Due to problems with education some executives had left their families in Japan.

In other cases parents have taken the decision to send their children to fee paying Japanese schools such as Rikkyo High School in Sussex, and the Gyosei International School in Milton Keynes. Such schools have the traditional Japanese curriculum. In spite of these problems, one Japanese executive did point to one positive factor for his children in a local school: 'In Japan foreign children in a school would be separated. My children go to a Cardiff school, and they are integrated in. For our children this is very acceptable.' Where children had been brought to Wales, and put into local secondary and primary schools then great use is made of the additional facilities provided by the Saturday morning schools which have been set up with the aid of the Wales–Japan Club.

The Saturday morning school at Whitchurch in Cardiff caters for just over 100 children between the ages of 7 and 15, i.e. the age at which they would attend elementary and junior high school in Japan. The school runs from 9.00 am until 3.00 pm. The school is divided into nine forms, three at junior high school level, and six at elementary level. There are seven teachers. In the morning pupils study the Japanese language, and in the afternoon they study mathematics. The practical running of the school is very much a joint venture between a number of companies, although Sony have provided accommodation and facilities, and Matsushita have provided some teachers.

However, even with this additional training, pupils returning to Japan face considerable handicaps when reintegrating into the education system with its emphasis on rigorous learning and discipline. The problems are worse for children in particular age groups, and worst of all for children who have been born in Wales and who have never experienced Japan. Furthermore, returning Japanese parents are often keen that their children do not lose the English-language skills acquired whilst in the UK, and are in some cases prepared to send children for regular extra tuition to maintain these skills. Thus the burden on the returnee children is great, and the problems of reintegration have sometimes been of a great enough magnitude for returning Japanese executives to leave their children in the UK to complete their higher education.

The case of two Japanese children who did not return to Japan were mentioned in the HTV documentary on the relationship between Japan and Wales entitled *The Dragon and the Rising Sun*.[1] Takeshi Tokita and Naoka Murata were both children of Japanese managing directors who had prolonged stays within Wales. During the programme Tokita said:

> I was thrown into school and I could not speak a word of English . . . but the people around me treated me the same . . . in about a month I picked the language up. I've been very fortunate that I have had the chance to go through the whole British system.

Such sentiments were echoed by Miss Murata, who was 14 when she had come to Wales, and had attended Brecon High School, before going on to graduate from the Royal Academy of Music: 'I felt sorry for myself being taken to Britain, having to say goodbye to all my friends, but looking back I've been lucky to have had this experience'.

There is some evidence that attitudes in Japan are changing towards young returnees. Returnee children are perceived as being different from other Japanese children, and are thought to be more 'individualistic, creative and broad minded'. In the 1970s Goodman felt that these values were held to be very un-Japanese because they came into conflict with the ideas of conformity, groupism and homogeneity that had maintained post-war Japanese growth.[2] More recently such children have been accorded a more positive status. Goodman notes that some Japanese universities now have quota systems to accept returnee children, and that some companies have actively recruited such children hoping that their creative skills may be positively used.

Few managers specifically commented that they were having problems getting Japanese food. Only one manager in North Wales commented that, 'food was lousy' and that 'the WDA should open a Japanese restaurant'. Several managers did say that they were able to make use of deliveries of Japanese food from London. A refrigerated van regularly toured Japanese plants in Wales. Few other problems were mentioned. In summary, it seemed that Japanese executives were enjoying the Welsh posting, and were making the most of the unique opportunities offered in the principality, but what was the impact of the posting on their longer term careers?

Impact on careers

Japanese managers generally felt that a posting in Wales had a positive impact on their careers and experience. A number of managers for example specifically noted that their spheres of responsibility and function were much wider whilst working in the subsidiary company. The following comments from managers show this:

> Our job here is far 'bigger' than in Japan where I would be limited to finance – here we have more management power – wider thinking and wider spheres. To encourage capability being in an overseas company is a good chance for us . . . Here (Wales) you can broaden your experience, you can do everything. In Japan your area is very limited – here in UK you have to do much more – this deepens experience and builds up your character.

A Japanese managing director in North Wales felt that a posting overseas provided different experiences, and that the experience of foreign lands might aid future promotion. A Japanese personnel director in South Wales said that in his company Japanese personnel positively welcomed their first overseas posting. At the same time other managers, whilst acknowledging positive aspects about the Welsh posting, also commented on possible problems. One Japanese technical manager had been away from Japan for over five years:

> I started work for the Japanese company in 1980, after graduating from university. I worked for three years in the maintenance department, then the company prepared me to go to Holland . . . My major job was to train local staff . . . I also helped in the building of a new factory. I went back to Japan for three months for further training in the latest technology then came here (Wales) 18 month ago . . . It's difficult to catch up with what's happened in Japan while I've been away, they all do R&D and develop so quickly. So it's very difficult to decide . . . to stay overseas or settle back in Japan.

Another managing director in a South Wales company also commented: 'It's a very good experience of a broader range of functions than we do in Japan. The danger is spending too long here and getting stuck.'

Within the Japanese parent companies, when graduates are initially recruited into a larger firm, they are circulated amongst a number of departments. Then after a period of five to ten years a specialism will develop. A subsidiary posting allowed managers in some cases to come out of their specialisms and fulfil more of a generalist role. Local managers have often been amazed at the versatility of expatriate staff across narrow functional boundaries.

Overall, the impact on careers was perceived as positive. Two managers in a recently established Japanese components maker in North Wales felt that in coming to Wales, expatriate personnel were showing a pioneering spirit for which they would be rewarded. This evidence is in some contrast to earlier studies. White, who examined the experiences of returning Japanese executives, found that they were often given little welcome and were placed within international sections of parent company businesses which had lesser status than main offices.[3] According to White such returnees were pawns in Japanese overseas expansion, permitting parent companies to make contact overseas, whilst not becoming contaminated by the outside world. Clearly, the evidence from Wales suggests that experience overseas is regarded as a career asset.

Japan meets Wales

The presence of Japanese manufacturing investment has created more than just an economic effect in Wales. Japanese involvement in the Welsh economy has contributed to a growing local interest in

Japanese life, language and culture, and to the development of educational and sporting links. In this section a sketch is provided of these developing ties which have done much to cement relationships between the two nations.

There has been a substantial interest in the Japanese language in Wales over the past ten years. As Japan has become a driving force in world trade, the ability to speak Japanese has become an important asset in commercial and industrial circles. In addition Japanese language skills contribute significantly to an understanding of Japanese society, history and culture. Local interest in the Japanese language is widespread. The Japanese evening class at the Whitchurch Adult Education Centre in Cardiff has been running for nearly ten years under the supervision of Ms Midori Matsui of the Takiron company. Over this time many students have passed through its beginners, intermediate and advanced courses. The Centre not only provides language teaching, but also gives insights into more general aspects of Japanese society and culture. More recently the Japanese Studies Centre at the University of Wales College of Cardiff (of which more below) has set up an intensive twelve week introduction to Japanese class, aimed at those in business and industry.

Interest in the Japanese language has not been limited to adults. For some years there has been scattered interest in bringing Japanese onto school curricula in Wales. Such efforts have gained support from the Secretary of State for Wales, who in 1989 provided financial support for a Japanese in Schools Programme. The further initial growth of the programme was aided by sponsorship from the Wales–Japan Club, the Daiwa Anglo–Japanese Foundation the GB–Sasakawa Foundation and the Japan Foundation. The aim of this programme has been to introduce Japanese language teaching into as many interested Welsh schools as possible at sixth-form level, and to guarantee the quality of teaching materials and courses offered at schools. The scheme is at present coming to the end of its first phase. At the end of the first year 11 schools and 70 students were participating in the programme, which involved three Japanese language teachers serving consortia of three or four schools each. The three consortia become self-financing in mid-1992. During mid-1992 another consortium of schools in Dyfed will join the programme which is coordinated by Ms Trixi Greenhough who is based at the Japanese Studies Centre at the University in Cardiff. To date the pilot schemes have been run among schools in Gwynedd, Mid- and South Glamorgan. In addition to the normal teaching, a two-day course, funded by TVEI Wales, was organized in March 1992: 40 students and 10 staff met at Gregynog near Newtown for intensive Japanese language sessions and hands-on cultural demonstrations for all of the participating schools.

The teaching of Japanese in Wales took a decisive step forward with the decision taken in 1988, and the opening in 1989, of the Japanese Studies Centre of the University of Wales College of Cardiff. Students of Japanese follow a four-year course, the third year of which is spent in Japan. Students receive an intensive course in the Japanese language, where equal attention is given to the ability to converse and to the mastery of Japan's uniquely complex writing system. By the time they graduate, those who have followed the course are equipped to take positions in industry, commerce, finance, education, government, etc., where they can use their knowledge of Japanese in a professional capacity.

Teaching at the Japanese Studies Centre is organized within a joint honours framework, so that besides the study of the Japanese language, its history, politics, economics, etc., students are able also to study either law, business studies or a European language together with Japanese. This enhances the academic scope of the degree and puts the study of Japan into international perspective, whilst at the same time increasing the vocational utility of the degree programme.

Whilst the majority of the teaching staff are native speakers of Japanese, so allowing students ample opportunity to practice their oral/aural skills, fundamental importance attaches to the year of study spent in Japan. The Centre has concluded formal arrangements with three Japanese universities, and discussions with others are also taking place. The three are Chuo University in Tokyo, Obirin University, also in Tokyo, and the University of Kitakyushu. The choice of host university for individual students depends on the subject studied with Japanese. When attending university in Japan, students follow advanced courses in Japanese and attend lectures and seminars on various aspects of Japanese culture and society. Students reading business studies with Japanese also undergo a three-month period of placement with companies located near their host university so as to experience at first hand the reality of Japanese industrial and commercial life.

The Cardiff Japanese Studies Centre is already the second largest university teaching department of Japanese in the United Kingdom and one of the best equipped. It also serves the Welsh economy by running a unit which offers a number of services to the business community. Besides intensive language courses run in the evenings, these include translation and interpreting services, as well as briefings on the various difficulties associated with doing business with Japan or visiting or living there.

The nature of links between Japan and Wales in educational terms is growing quickly in diversity. A link between Wales and Japan has been forged by Hiroshi Mizutani of the Kinjo Gakuin private university in Nagoya. Following an initial visit to Wales in the 1970s, Professor Mizutani returned in the 1980s and learnt Welsh under an intensive ULPAN scheme. Mizutani has been involved in Japan in the setting up of a Celtic Congress and a Japanese Society of Welsh Studies. Lecturers from Aberystwyth and Lampeter have been to Japan to speak at this congress.

Links are also being forged between some Welsh schools and their Japanese counterparts. For example, Heolddu school is twinned with Maebashi Nishi High School. During 1990 a party of students from the Japanese school came over to have a taste of the Welsh way of life. During 1991 students from the Heolddu school went out to Japan. There is also a twinning arrangement between Glantaf, Cardiff's Welsh-medium secondary school, and a school in Shimitzu city in Japan. This link was brought about by a Welsh speaking teacher in the Japanese school, Tsutomo Iyanagi. Pupils in the Japanese school are compiling a Welsh–Japanese dictionary, and the schools hope to arrange mutual student visits.

Cultural understanding of Japan received a boost during 1991 with the coming of the Japan Festival to Wales. This was part of the nationwide Japan Festival which featured over 300 national events at a cost of £10 million. Within Wales the Japan Festival ran from August 1991 to January 1992, and featured over fifty special events. There were a series of musical events. These included a concert by the Tokyo Symphony Orchestra at Swansea and special concerts featuring noted Japanese musicians throughout Wales. The BBC Welsh Symphony Orchestra gave a concert of the work of the famous living Japanese composer Takemitsu.

Crafts and visual arts also played a prominent part in the Festival, with an exhibition of contemporary Japanese art *Radicalchip* throughout Cardiff venues. In other parts of Wales there were exhibitions of Japanese ceramics, woodcuts, kite making and lantern making. A bonsai exhibition was held at Duffryn Gardens in Cardiff. A series of special Japan Weeks at St. Donats, Pontypridd, and Caernarfon provided interactive workshops allowing schoolchildren the opportunity to have hands on experience of Japanese calligraphy, origami, drumming, story-telling and Japanese crafts. Performing arts also played a part in the Japan Festival Wales. The Kikunokai company gave performances of traditional Japanese dance and drum in Swansea. There was also a Kabuki Hamlet and Lear at Cardiff.

South Glamorgan County Council has active links with Fukuoka prefecture in Japan. During the Festival these links were consolidated with an exhibition of living arts and crafts from Fukuoka in Cardiff. Japanese craftsmen from Fukuoka came to Cardiff to work on and display Hakata Dolls, Yame Tops, Sawara Ceramics and Hakata Scissors. Perhaps the highlight of the Japan Festival in Wales was the exhibition of Yabusame (Japanese horseback archery) at Bute Park in Cardiff.

The Festival was unique in that it covered the whole of Wales, and had events that appealed to those of all age groups. It was an important development in bridging the cultural divide between Wales and Japan, and had the sponsorship of not only a number of Japanese companies in Wales, through the Wales–Japan Club, but also a number of locally based firms and organizations including county councils, banks, companies and development agencies. The large degree of practical support for the Festival showed an awareness of the importance of developing deeper links with Japan.

Closer links between Wales and Japan have also been consolidated through sport. Rugby union is perhaps the best example. Rugby has been played in Japan for nearly a century. During 1973 the Japanese national side toured Wales, bringing with them 200 supporters. A number of these supporters were so kindly treated during their short stay that they formed the Japan–Wales Rugby Club, and have continued to return to the region ever since.

There are now also opportunities for the Welsh to sample the very different Japanese cuisine. For some years there has been a traditional Japanese restaurant at Felin Geri near Newcastle

Emlyn. The restaurant is decorated as an old Japanese village inn, with wooden tables and benches, stone floors, open fires and authentic Japanese table wear and utensils. A Japanese chef provides the traditional food. In addition, Cardiff now has a Japanese restaurant run by Mrs Chikako Cameron. This has only recently opened, and at present 50 per cent of the clients of the 'Chikako' restaurant are Japanese. However, Mrs Cameron hopes that local people will increasingly be tempted by the novel Japanese cuisine on offer.

There is little doubt that the presence of so large a concentration of Japanese manufacturing investment has in no small part brought Japan closer to Wales in terms of mutual understanding and appreciation. This is something that the individual Japanese companies in Wales have been keen to encourage, not only through the sponsorship of activities such as the Japan festival, but also through the gradual development of a network of linkages with their respective local communities. Many of the Japanese plants are in their initial stages of development and it is hoped that their linkages in the local community will grow as they expand their local manufacturing operations. For the Japanese personnel in Wales, the tour of duty appears to be perceived as a valuable career step. In spite of initial settling-in difficulties, and some fears about the education of children, returning Japanese leave the principality reluctantly, and with good memories of their limited stay.

Conclusions

The objective of this volume was to present a comprehensive picture of the economic, social and cultural consequences of Japanese manufacturing investment for Wales and its people. It has been shown that the consequences have been greater than one would perhaps expect given the small comparative size of the investments to date.

Undoubtedly, Wales would be a poorer place without the Japanese. The local economy has benefited from the direct employment created, and from the growing number of purchasing linkages that the Japanese have developed in Wales. Further, continued Japanese expansions in the late 1980s and early 1990s have lessened Welsh dependence on North America as a source of investment, and have contributed to sectoral diversification of the narrow Welsh manufacturing base. Ultimately, however, the economic analysis of the Japanese contribution poses as many questions as it does answers. In this book we have questioned both the nature and quality of employment provision, together with the characteristics of plant operations. These are standard criticisms which also apply to regional concentrations of foreign inward investment from other parent economies.

These questions lead on to a consideration of the extent to which Wales has been chosen by the Japanese as simply a least-cost production location, with the advantage of access to adjacent markets. General empirical evidence considering the determinants of Welsh shares of new incoming foreign direct investment suggests that production-cost considerations have been important. If production cost minimization *is* a key motivation, then there is the possibility that future projects will be directed to other areas of the European fringe where production costs can be even further lowered, but access to the core EC market still gained. To date however, employment in Japanese subsidiaries in Wales has grown rapidly. This has been the case even during the midst of a recession that has seen demand for the type of electronic consumer goods made in Wales fall drastically.

Regional development is far more than just a question of economics and employment. Whilst some elements of the economic impact of Japanese plants have been quantifiable, the social and cultural consequences are less easily measured. Yet, it is in terms of social consequences that the 'Japanese effect' is most noticeable. When the initial Japanese manufacturers entered Wales during the 1970s they were perceived as being different. Nowhere more has this been shown to be the case than in their work-organization and personnel-management practices. One objective of the regional policy that played such an important part in bringing the Japanese to Wales, was that such inward investment should provide a stimulus for new management ideas. The larger Japanese electronics manufacturers in Wales have provided showcase examples of new forms of operational management with an emphasis on quality throughout. Systems of work organization and workforce control focus around ensuring final product quality, as do systems that emphasize an accelerated flow of materials and components through production plants. The Japanese preoccupation with total quality has also pervaded personnel practices, particularly staff selection, training, appraisal, discipline and communications. It is in no small way due to the changed work organization and personnel practices that Welsh employees have developed a 'Japanese-style' of working, centring on individual responsibility for product quality, team working and functional flexibility.

This new working system has been made possible by a new industrial relations climate within the Japanese plants. This remains one of the most significant consequences of the Japanese presence. The Japanese preference for single union agreements, sought through 'beauty parades', together with the inter-union recognition battles played out in Japanese subsidiaries during the 1980s, have led to an acceptance of strike-free deals which have inexorably affected industrial relations practices and the industrial-relations environment not just in Wales but throughout the UK.

Finally, it was possible to show that the Japanese presence has had a significant community and cultural dimension. The larger Japanese manufacturing subsidiaries are now amongst the largest employers within their respective communities, and are beginning to play a corporate-citizen role through the development of linkages with schools, colleges, TECs, charities and sports organizations. The skills that are embodied within Japanese enterprise are thus gradually being applied to challenges in the wider Welsh community and society.

The high public profile given to the Japanese subsidiaries has also aided a greater understanding of Japanese business and culture among the Welsh people more generally. In consequence cultural, educational, and sporting ties between the two nations are growing rapidly.

In concluding, although Japanese enterprise only accounts for just over 1 per cent of total Welsh employment at 1993, its economic and social impact in particular has been significant. But what of the future? At the time of writing the Japanese economy is experiencing a rapid deceleration in its pace of growth, and business confidence has been correspondingly affected. Many large Japanese corporations are reporting lower profits, and stock prices have fallen during 1992/93. Uncertainties in the Japanese economy have left capital investment low, and the main Japanese economic indicators suggest that at 1993 the Japanese economy is facing a period of difficult adjustment. Conditions in the home economy will ultimately affect the overseas operations of Japanese multinationals.

The Japanese economic situation, coupled with recession in European consumer markets, has meant in practice that Japanese subsidiaries in Wales have either placed expansion plans back, or in some circumstances have revised spending plans. In spite of this, it is expected that employment within Japanese subsidiaries will continue to grow at a steady level over the next few years, reaching around 17,000 by 1995.

It is clear that the boom in Japanese investment that occurred during the mid-to late 1980s is largely over. The boom in new job creation was largely down to expansion projects among Japanese firms who had arrived in Wales in thc 1970s and early 1980s. In fact the bulk of new job creation has been concentrated among only 8 of the 29 Japanese manufacturing subsidiaries in Wales. Large new greenfield projects with substantial long-term job creating potential are becoming fewer and further between. The recent Sony investment at Pencoed near Bridgend, bringing the Sony Welsh workforce to around 4,000 people, was a considerable coup, but it is unlikely that such large investments will feature strongly in the future, at least within the present economic climate. A great deal of press comment has centred around the Toyota engine plant at Deeside in North Wales. But regrettably this is not a car plant, and even at full capacity it is doubtful if employment will exceed 300 people even by 1995. The bulk of recent Japanese investments in greenfield terms have been in the components industry including makers of plastic mouldings, electronic harnesses and electronic components and piece parts. Whilst employment in these plants has been significant, it does not come anywhere near the employment provision of the larger plants.

Looking a little further ahead there is perhaps a developing problem in the extent to which existing Japanese investment in Wales is essentially concentrated in a narrow industry segment, i.e. consumer electronics goods and office automation equipment. Within Wales there is beginning to develop a supply infrastructure to serve those large Japanese electronics goods makers who came to Wales during the 1970s and early 1980s, such as Sony, Sharp, Brother and Matsushita. Several of the incoming Japanese component makers are heavily dependent on these firms. There arises then the spectre that at some future time if and when the large Japanese electronics manufacturers cease trading in Wales, that the direct effects of closures will be compounded by indirect consequences.

In the context of a regional development strategy this is no time for Wales to settle back. True, Wales has been successful in attracting a high proportion of the Japanese manufacturing investment to enter the UK to date, but further effort is needed. Coupled with attempts to attract inward investment from other geographical origins, there is a need for Japanese investments in other product areas. Recent investments by Japanese automobile/automobile components makers such as Toyota, Calsonic and Lucas-SEI have been valuable additions to the local economy, reinforcing the significant motor industry presence in Wales. However other sectors remain unrepresented – including pharmaceuticals, machine tools, integrated circuits, food and general manufacturing. If the attraction of Japanese overseas investment is to remain important in policy terms, then over-concentration in narrow product bands should be avoided if the painful structural readjustments that have dogged Wales in the past are to be avoided.

The ultimate concern of Japanese management in Wales has been the quality of the final product. The concern for Wales on the other hand is the quality of inward investment. Wales not only requires new Japanese industrial sectors to come to Wales but also requires functional diversification from the investors already present. Regrettably, very few of the Japanese operations include either higher control functions, research or design. Some of the longer established manufacturers are beginning to do some research and development locally. Perhaps the best example is Sony, which has made a positive commitment to designing and developing colour television sets and components at Bridgend. Unfortunately, Sony is not a typical Japanese firm, and few other investors have as yet followed in its footsteps. Without the presence of more self-determination and higher engineering and design functions both the economic and social consequences of the investments will be significantly reduced in the future. In this respect one key recent development has been the increasing popularity of joint ventures including Gooding–Sanken, Dowty–Koike and Lucas–SEI. Such agreements may provide added opportunities for technology transfer, coupled with a greater element of self-determination at the local level.

The future development of Japanese manufacturing in Wales depends on factors both within and without the control of the corporations themselves. Whilst questions remain concerning economic contribution, there is little doubt that in a relatively short time Japanese manufacturers in Wales have become increasingly important players in the local economy and society.

Notes

One: Japanese Investment in Wales: The Backcloth

1. P. Dicken, 'The changing geography of Japanese foreign direct investment in manufacturing industry: a global perspective', in J. Morris (ed.), *Japan and the Global Economy*, London, Routledge, 1991, 14–44.
2. H. Itami, 'Globalization of Japanese firms and their challenges', Paper presented to Global Kaisha Conference, Manchester, June 1992.
3. T. Morris-Suzuki, 'Reshaping the international division of labour: Japanese manufacturing investment in South-east Asia', in J. Morris (ed.), *Japan and the Global Economy*, London, Routledge, 1991, 135–153.
4. T. Ozawa, 'Technical alliances of Japanese firms: an "industrial restructuring" account of the latest phase of capitalist development', Paper presented at the Symposium of New Technology, Technical Alliances and Social Innovations Within the Enterprise, Université du Quebec, Montreal, October 1992.
5. K. Ohmae, *The Borderless World*, London, Collins, 1990.
6. See, for example, J. Morris, 'Globalization and global localization: explaining trends in Japanese foreign manufacturing investment', in J. Morris (ed.), 1991, 1–13.
7. W. Emmott, *The Sun Also Sets: Why Japan Will Not Be Number One*, London, Economist Publications, 1989. See also W. Emmott, *Japan's Global Reach*, London, Century Press, 1992.
8. See K. Kojima, *Japan and the New World Economic Order*, London, Croom Helm, 1977; T. Ozawa, 'International investment and industrial structure: new theoretical implications from the Japanese experience', *Oxford Economic Papers N.S.*, 1970, 72–9.

9. J. E. Roemer, 'Japanese direct investment in manufacturing: some comparisons with the US pattern', *Quarterly Review of Economics and Business*, 1976, 91–111.
10. Japanese External Trade Organization (JETRO), reported in M. Kamamoto, 'Investment in manufacturing: Time for rigorous assessment', *Financial Times*, Japan and the European Community Supplement, 13 November 1992, 3.
11. J. Morris, *Japanese Investment in the EEC*, Report to DG1, EC, Brussels, 1987.
12. Invest in Britain Bureau, *Annual Report*, London, Invest in Britain Bureau, 1991: Invest in Britain Bureau, *Annual Report*, London, Invest in Britain Bureau, 1992.
13. J. Dunning, *Japanese Participation in British Industry*, London, Croom Helm, 1986.
14. J. Morris, 'The who, why and where of Japanese manufacturing investment in the UK', *Industrial Relations Journal*, 19 (1), 1988, 31–40. M. Munday, *Japanese Manufacturing Investment in Wales*, Cardiff, University of Wales Press, 1990.

Two: Japanese Investment in Wales: The Who, Why and What

1. Arthur D. Little, *A Report on the Japanese Experience in Wales*, Cardiff, WDA, 1986; M. Munday, *Japanese Manufacturing Investment in Wales*, Cardiff, University of Wales Press, 1990; J. Morris, *Japanese Investment in the EEC: The Effects of Integration*, Report to DGI, EEC, Brussels, 1987; J. Morris, 'The Japanese are here – for better or worse?', *Welsh Economic Review*, 1 (2), 47–9, 1988; A. Moreton, 'Welsh question value of Japanese investment', *The Financial Times*, 13 June 1988, 1.
2. See, for example, A. Cawson, K. Morgan, D. Webber, P. Holmes and A. Stevens, *Hostile Brothers: Competition and Closure in the European Electronics Industry*, Oxford, Clarendon Press., 1991.
3. Arthur D. Little, 1986, *op. cit.*, Munday, 1990, *op. cit.*, Morris, 1988, *op. cit.*
4. J. Morris and R. Imrie, *Transforming Buyer–Supplier Relations: Japanese Industrial Practices in a Western Context*, London, Macmillan, 1992.
5. J. Dunning, *Japanese Participation in British Industry*, Beckenham, Kent, Croom Helm, 1986; Arthur D. Little, 1986, *op. cit.*
6. Morris, 1988, *op. cit.*
7. Morris, 1988, *op. cit.*
8. Morris, 1988, *op. cit.*

9. K. Williams, C. Haslam, J. Williams, A. Adcroft and S. Johal, *Factories or Warehouses?: Japanese Manufacturing Direct Investment in Britain and the United States*, Occasional Papers on Business Economy and Society, 6, London, Polytechnic of East London, 1992.
10. Morris, 1988, *op. cit.*

Three: Japanese Manufacturing Investments in Wales: The Economic Consequences

1. See *Regional Trends*, 25, 1991.
2. S. Hill and M. Munday, 'Why are Welsh wages so low?', *Welsh Economic Review*, 4(1), Spring 1991, 58.
3. D. Simpson, 'Why are Welsh wages so low II?', *Welsh Economic Review*, 5(1), Spring 1992, 63.
4. S. Hill and M. Munday, 'Foreign direct investment in Wales', *Local Economy*, 6(1), May 1991, 22.
5. Welsh Affairs Committee, *Inward Investment into Wales and its Interaction with Regional and EEC Policies*, Minutes of Evidence 22.2.88 and First Report 14.12.88, London, HMSO.
6. S. Hill and M. Munday, 'The regional distribution of FDI within the UK', *Regional Studies*, 26(6), 1992, 535–544.
7. Hill and Munday, *Local Economy*, 1991, *op. cit.*, 31–2.
8. Our findings are based on our major study in 1992, and we are confident in the accuracy of our figures.
9. See for example G. Davies and I. Thomas, *Overseas Investment in Wales*, Swansea, C. Davies, 1976.
10. See *Welsh Economic Trends,* 1992.
11. Hill and Munday, *Local Economy*, 1991, *op. cit.*, 33.
12. S. Young, 'Scotland v Wales in the inward investment game', *Quarterly Economic Commentary*, 14(3), 1989, 59–63.
13. Intermatrix Limited, *Market Opportunities for Electronic Component Manufacturers*, London, DTI, 1991.
14. *Ibid.*
15. Correspondence with A. Abbott, Director CTV Operations (Sony Bridgend), 16 May 1990.
16. For details of this survey, and resulting work see M. Munday, 'The financial consequences of linkages with Japanese manufacturers', *Management Accounting*, 68(7), 1990, 42–43; and M. Munday, 'Integrated materials management–beyond component quality', *Logistics Today*, 10(4), 1991, 23–5.
17. Munday, 1990, *op. cit.*
18. M. Munday, *Japanese Manufacturing Investment in Wales*, Cardiff University of Wales Press, 1990.

19. Letter from a former Sony manager to *The Financial Times*, 22 January 1991.
20. Japanese External Trade Organization Report, *Current Management Situation of Japanese Manufacturing Enterprises in Europe*, JETRO London, Research Division, March 1992.
21. Young, 1989, *op. cit.*

Four: Work, Organization and Management

1. There are many detailed accounts of JIT and TQC. For a summary see N. Oliver and B. Wilkinson, *The Japanization of British Industry*, 2nd Edn., Oxford, Blackwell, 1992.
2. For an account of the origins of JIT at Toyota see M. Cusumano, *The Japanese Automobile Industry: Technology and Management at Nissan and Toyota*, Cambridge, MA, Harvard University Press, 1986.
3. Such an organizational form, because of its ability to function effectively with relatively few indirect staffs, has been characterized as a 'lean production' system. For a popular and influential account of the assumed superiority of 'lean production', see J.P. Womack, D.T. Jones and D. Roos, *The Machine that Changed the World: The Triumph of Lean Production*, New York, Rawson Macmillan, 1990.
4. P. Wickens, *The Road to Nissan,* London, Macmillan, 1987.
5. S. C. Kolm, 'Must one be Buddhist to grow? an analysis of the cultural basis of Japanese productivity', in P. Koslowski (ed.), *Economics and Philosophy*, Tubingen, J.C.B. Mohr, 1985, 221–42.
6. For a discussion of *kaizen* and work intensification see R. Delbridge, P. Turnbull and B. Wilkinson, 'Work intensification and management control under JIT/TQC production regimes', *New Technology, Work and Employment*, September 1992.
7. In the light of documenting such staffing practices in transplants in North America, one author refers to the system as 'management-by-stress'. See J. Slaughter, *The team concept in the US auto industry*. Paper presented to the Conference on the Japanization of British Industry, Cardiff Business School, 17–18 September 1987.
8. In one case a company allowed for 3.75 per cent above the calculated labour requirement, though actual absence figures were 4.25 per cent. Unfortunately we did not discover the extent to which other companies maintained discrepancies between calculated labour requirements and manning levels.
9. For a detailed discussion of surveillance under JIT/TQC production systems see G. Sewell and B. Wilkinson, 'Someone to watch over me: surveillance, discipline and the just-in-time labour process', *Sociology*, 26(2), 1992, 271–289.

10. In one large company from which we were given a breakdown of labour turnover figures for 1991, 33 out of 261 leavers had left after failing their probation for poor attendance, and 43 non-probationers were dismissed for poor absence/lateness records. A further 19 were dismissed for other reasons such as unacceptable performance. Commonly made statements from managers about the strictness of their systems of discipline, especially for absence, would suggest such figures are not untypical: unfortunately we were rarely allowed such turnover breakdowns, so we cannot provide a numerical demonstration.
11. Between 1979 and 1984 the factory was a GEC–Hitachi joint venture. Hitachi imposed a new management style when it took complete control. For a detailed account see T. Pegge, *UK management/union relations - Japanese style*, Trent Polytechnic Business School, Open Lecture, 13 November 1984.
12. *Western Mail*, 20 February 1988.
13. The subject of work ethics, work values and work attitudes in Japan is one which draws a wide variety of interpretations. For two extremes see M. Morishima, *Why Has Japan Succeeded? Western Technology and the Japanese Ethos*, Cambridge, Cambridge University Press, 1982, which argues that a strong work ethic derives from a feudal legacy and Japanese Confucianism, and P. Briggs, 'The Japanese at work: illusions of the ideal', *Industrial Relations Journal*, 19 (1), 1988, 24–30, who argues that a variety of insidious control devices are used by companies to gain compliance. From Briggs's perspective, the Japanese employee working unpaid after the end of the shift is likely to be doing so under peer pressure or under the knowledge that management might sooner or later find means of penalizing employees - materially or through public humiliation - who do not demonstrate enthusiasm and commitment.
14. One company used the term 'senior hand' in preference to 'float', on the grounds that 'the company does not have floating labour - no one stands idle'.
15. This might help explain why, when we asked managers to describe their organization's culture, they would be likely to use terms like 'family atmosphere' and 'consensus decision making', but at the same time 'very strict' and 'on a scale of one to ten we're about six on autocratic'.
16. P. Wickens, 1987, *op. cit.*
17. Only time will tell whether internal promotion policies will lead to a tradition of home-grown senior managers in Japanese transplants in Wales. Our impression was that whilst company policies might encourage this, rapid expansion in the last few years, together with the

fact that managers here are more likely to be mobile across companies than their Japanese counterparts, have so far hindered such a development.

18. On returning to work his Japanese managing director joked with him that when the company was set up a few years ago, he should not have persuaded him not to implement compulsory exercises for all staff.
19. The 1,800 hour year for employees is the target established for Japanese corporations by the Japanese government in the light of international complaints of unfair competition. Critics of long working hours (many unpaid) in Japan claim 2,500 to 3,000 hours are not untypical and lead to serious stress-related illnesses. See National Defence Counsel for Victims of Karoshi, *Karoshi: When the Corporate Warrior Dies*, Tokyo, Mado-Sha, 1990.
20. *The Financial Times*, 22 November 1991.

Five: Personnel Management

1. There are many accounts of the Japanese employment system. For an overview and an account of its origins see C. R. Littler, *The Development of the Labour Process in Capitalist Societies*, London, Heinemann, 1982.
2. An equally interesting question might be whether the peripheral worker model has been transferred.
3. Acceptance of tight discipline is similarly documented with regard to women workers in Japanese electronics transplants in Britain and Ireland: see M. Saso, *Women in the Japanese Workplace*, London, Hilary Shipman, 1980.
4. Quoted in *Western Mail*, 14 September 1988.
5. V. Pucik, 'Managing Japan's white-collar workers', *Euro-Asia Business Review*, 4(3), 1985, 16–21.
6. Highly selective recruitment practices are reported in Japanese transplants across the UK: see M. White and M. Trevor, *Under Japanese Management: The Experience of British Workers*, London, Heinemann, 1983: and K. K. Pang and N. Oliver, 'Personnel strategy in eleven Japanese manufacturing companies in the UK', *Personnel Review*, 17(3), 1988, 16–21.
7. See L. Naylor, 'Bringing home the lessons', *Personnel Management* 16(3), 1984, 34–37; and J. Hirschmeier and T. Yui, *The Development of Japanese Business*, London, Allen & Unwin, 1981.
8. We do not necessarily intend to characterize Japanese management as being unique in this regard. Indeed, the flagship American corporation, IBM, has been described as 'the biggest boy scout troop in the world'.

9. See for instance, V. Pucik, M. Hanada and G. Fifield, *Management Culture and the Effectiveness of Local Executives and Japanese-Owned US Corporations*, New York, Egon Zehnder, 1989.
10. T. Pegge, 'UK management/union relations - Japanese style', Trent Polytechnic Business School, Open Lecture, 13 November 1984.
11. K. Endo, '*Satei* (personal assessment) and inter-worker competition in Japanese firms', Faculty of Economics, Yamagata University, Japan, unpublished paper.
12. Our findings on the use of appraisals in Japanese transplants in Wales largely concur with the findings of another Cardiff Business School study which documented similar practices in Japanese transplants across Britain. See C. Yu and B. Wilkinson, *Pay and Appraisal in Japanese Companies in Britain*, Japanese Management Research Unit Working Paper No.8, Cardiff Business School, UWCC, 1989.
13. T. Pegge, 1984, *op. cit.*

Six: Industrial Relations

1. For a discussion of the fragility of JIT systems of production and the consequences for power in organizations see B. Wilkinson and N. Oliver, 'Power, control and the *Kanban*', *Journal of Management Studies*, 26(1), 1989, 47–58.
2. For a good summary of industrial relations in Japan see J.S. Moore, 'Japanese industrial relations', *Labour and Industry*, 1(1), 1987, 140–155.
3. For insights into the fascinating history of labour relations in Japan see M. Cusumano, *The Japanese Automobile Industry: Technology and Management at Nissan and Toyota*, Cambridge, MA, Harvard University Press, 1986; C. R. Littler, *The Development of the Labour Process in Capitalist Societies*, London, Heinemann, 1982; M. Kenney and R. Florida, 'Beyond mass production: production and the labour process in Japan', *Politics and Society*, 16(1), 1988, 121–155; M. Morishima, *Why Has Japan Succeeded? Western Technology and the Japanese Ethos*, Cambridge, Cambridge University Press, 1982; and W. Dean Kinzley, Industrial Harmony in Modern Japan: The Invention of a Tradition, London, Routledge, 1991.
4. M. Munday, *Japanese Manufacturing Investment in Wales*, Cardiff, University of Wales Press, 1990.
5. *The Times*, 15 November 1976.
6. M. Munday, 1990, *op. cit.*
7. W Reitsperger, 'Japanese management: coping with British industrial relations', *Journal of Management Studies*, 23(1), 1986, 72–88.
8. *The Financial Times*, 30 December 1986.

9. *The Independent*, 31 March 1988. Author's original emphasis.
10. Wales TUC, General Council, *Wales TUC and Inward Investment*. Positional paper approved by the Wales TUC General Council, 8 July 1987.
11. *Ibid*.
12. *Ibid*.
13. *The Observer*, 21 February 1988.
14. ACAS/WINVEST, *Successful Industrial Relations: The Experience of Overseas Companies in Wales*, Cardiff, ACAS, Wales, 1986.
15. Wales TUC, General Council, 1987, *op. cit.*
16. *Western Mail*, 9 January 1992.
17. See P. Beaumont, *The Decline of Trade Union Organization*, London, Croom Helm, 1987; and P. Bassett, *Strike-Free: New Industrial Relations in Britain*, London, Macmillan, 1986.
18. T. Pegge, 'UK management/union relations – Japanese style', Trent Polytechnic Business School Open Lecture, 13 November 1984, 9.
19. *Ibid*.
20. *Ibid*. 14–15. Whether political ignorance or fear of the consequences of upsetting Hitachi, both of which are implied in these comments, were uppermost in the minds of workers accepting the single union deal, remains debatable, though later in the same paper (p.36) Pegge himself comments that: 'I have to admit . . . it has taken really a fair degree of fear that there was no alternative to be producing all of those changes so quickly.'
21. Munday, 1990, *op. cit.*
22. Pegge, 1984, *op. cit.*
23. It is worth pointing out here the confusion over pendulum and binding arbitration, which are in fact different concepts. Binding arbitration means just that – the arbitrator's decision is final. Pendulum arbitration means that the arbitrator is obliged to find wholly in favour of one side or the other; he cannot recommend a compromise position. Pendulum arbitration may or may not also be binding. The EETPU generally prefers pendulum *and* binding arbitration, hence the confusion.
24. *South Wales Echo*, 1 May 1987.
25. The speech was broadcast on *HTV News*, 24 May 1988.
26. *The Independent*, 7 July 1988.
27. *The Guardian*, 6 September 1988.
28. *Business Wales*, 14 January 1990.
29. See N. Oliver and B. Wilkinson, *The Japanization of British Industry*, 2nd edn., Oxford, Blackwell, 1992.
30. See *ibid*. for several examples.
31. W. Bevan, 'Creating a no-strike environment: the trade union view'. Speech given to a CBI Conference, 12 June 1987.

32. P. Wickens, *The Road to Nissan*, London, Macmillan, 1987.
33. There are, however, cases documented in other areas of the UK where other unions have conceded the first stage of bargaining to a consultative committee.
34. For a full discussion of the Company Advisory Board at Toshiba, see M. Trevor, *Toshiba's New British Company*, London, 1988.
35. T. Pegge, 'Hitachi two years on', *Personnel Management*, October 1986, 42–47.
36. *Ibid*.
37. See I. Linn, *Single Union Deals: A Case Study of the Norsk Hydro Plant at Immingham, Humberside*, Barnsley, Northern College and TGWU Region 10, 1986, for a detailed discussion of the dilemmas for trade unions posed by members boards.
38. Bevan, 1987, *op. cit.*
39. Section 18 of the Trade Union and Labour Relations Act enables collective agreements to be registered as legally binding. However, this provision has rarely been used, and as far as we are aware none of the collective agreements signed between Japanese companies and unions in Wales have been made legally enforceable.
40. *The Guardian*, 6 September 1988.
41. Quoted in P. Bassett, *Strike-Free: New Industrial Relations in Britain*, London, Macmillan, 1986, 2.
42. *The Financial Times*, 20 January 1988.
43. M. Gregory, 'The no-strike deal in action', *Personnel Management*, December 1986, 30–33.
44. *Personnel Today*, 19 April 1988.
45. This dispute, trivial as it appears in retrospect, hit the headlines in Wales: see *South Wales Echo*, 26 June 1987.

Seven: Japan in Wales: Japanese Manufacturing and the Welsh Community

1. *The Dragon and the Rising Sun*, HTV, TV Centre, Culverhouse Cross. Written and produced by M. Slater, 1991.
2. R. Goodman, 'The Japanese abroad: a new class emerging?', *Anglo-Japanese Economic Review*, 3 (4), 1990, 13–14.
3. M. White, *The Japanese Overseas: Can They Go Home Again?*, New York, Free Press, 1988, quoted in Goodman, 1990, *op. cit.*, 14.

Bibliography

ACAS/WINvest, *Successful Industrial Relations: The Experience of Overseas Companies in Wales*, Cardiff, ACAS, Wales, 1986.

Anglo-Japanese Journal, 6(1), May 1992.

P. Bassett, *Strike-Free: New Industrial Relations in Britain*, London, Macmillan, 1986.

P. Beaumont, *The Decline of Trade Union Organization*, London, Croom Helm, 1987.

W. Bevan, 'Creating a no-strike environment: the trade union view'. Speech given to a CBI Conference, 12 June 1987.

P. Briggs, 'The Japanese at work: illusions of the ideal', *Industrial Relations Journal*, 19(1), 1988, 24–30.

Business Wales, various issues.

A. Cawson, K. Morgan, D. Webber, P. Holmes and A. Stevens, *Hostile Brothers: Competition and Closure in the European Electronics Industry*, Oxford, Clarendon Press, 1991.

M. Cusumano, *The Japanese Automobile Industry: Technology and Management at Nissan and Toyota*, Cambridge, MA, Harvard University Press, 1986.

G. Davies and I. Thomas, *Overseas Investment in Wales*, Swansea, C. Davies, 1976.

R. Delbridge, P. Turnbull and B. Wilkinson, 'Work intensification and management control under JIT/TQC production regimes,' *New Technology, Work and Employment*, 7(2), 1992, 97–106.

P. Dicken, 'The changing geography of Japanese foreign direct investment in manufacturing industry: a global perspective', in J. Morris (ed.), *Japan and the Global Economy*, London, Routledge, 1991, 14–44.

The Dragon and the Rising Sun, HTV, TV Centre, Culverhouse Cross, written and produced by M. Slater, 1991.

J. Dunning, *Japanese Participation in British Industry*, London, Croom Helm, 1986.

W. Emmott, *The Sun Also Sets: Why Japan Will Not Be Number One*, London, Economist Publications, 1989.

W. Emmott, *Japan's Global Reach*, London, Century Press, 1992.

K. Endo, '*Satei* [personal assessment] and inter-worker competition in Japanese firms', Faculty of Economics, Yamagata University, Japan, unpublished paper.

The Financial Times, various issues.

R. Goodman, 'The Japanese abroad: a new class emerging?', *Anglo-Japanese Economic Review*, 3(4), 1990, 13–14.

M. Gregory, 'The no-strike deal in action', *Personnel Management*, December 1986, 30–3.

The Guardian, various issues.

S. Hill and M. Munday, 'Why are Welsh wages so low?', *Welsh Economic Review*, 4(1), Spring 1991, 58.

S. Hill and M. Munday, 'Foreign direct investment in Wales', *Local Economy*, 6(1), 1991, 22.

S. Hill and M. Munday, 'The regional distribution of FDI within the UK', *Regional Studies*, 26(6), 1992, 535–44.

J. Hirschmeier and T. Yui, *The Development of Japanese Business*, London, Allen & Unwin, 1981.

Intermatrix Limited, *Market Opportunities for Electronic Component Manufacturers*, London, DTI, 1991.

The Independent, various issues.

Invest in Britain Bureau, *Annual Report*, London, Invest in Britain Bureau, 1991.

Invest in Britain Bureau, *Annual Report*, London, Invest in Britain Bureau, 1992.

H. Itami, 'Globalization of Japanese firms and their challenges,' Paper presented to Global Kaisha Conference, Manchester, June 1992.

Japanese External Trade Organisation Report, *Current Management Situation of Japanese Manufacturing Enterprises in Europe*, JETRO London, Research Division, March 1992.

M. Kamamoto, 'Investment in manufacturing: time for rigorous assessment' – *Financial Times*, Japan and the European Community Supplement, 13 November 1992, 3.

M. Kenney and R. Florida, 'Beyond mass production: production and the labour process in Japan', *Politics and Society*, 16(1), 1988, 121–55.

W. Dean Kinzley, *Industrial Harmony in Modern Japan: The Invention of a Tradition*, London, Routledge, 1991.

K. Kojima, *Japan and the New World Economic Order*, London, Croom Helm, 1977.

S. C. Kolm, 'Must one be Buddhist to grow? An analysis of the cultural basis of Japanese productivity', in P. Koslowski (ed.), *Economics and Philosophy*, Tubingen, J. C. B. Mohr, 1985, 221–42.

I. Linn, *Single Union Deals: A Case Study of the Norsk Hydro Plant at Immingham, Humberside*, Barnsley, Northern College and TGWU Region 10, 1986.

Arthur D. Little, *A Report on the Japanese Experience in Wales*, Cardiff, WDA, 1986.

C. R. Littler, *The Development of the Labour Process in Capitalist Societies*, London, Heinemann, 1982.

J. S. Moore, 'Japanese industrial relations', *Labour and Industry*, 1(1), 1987, 140–55.

A. Moreton, 'Welsh question value of Japanese investment', *The Financial Times*, 13 June 1988, 1.

M. Morishima, *Why Has Japan Succeeded? Western Technology and the Japanese Ethos*, Cambridge, Cambridge University Press, 1982.

J. Morris, *Japanese Investment in the EEC*, Report to DGI, EC, Brussels, 1987.

J. Morris, 'The who, why and where of Japanese manufacturing investment in the UK', *Industrial Relations Journal*, 19(1), 1988, 31–40.

J. Morris, 'Globalization and global localization: explaining trends in Japanese foreign manufacturing investment', in J. Morris (ed.) *Japan and the Global Economy*, London, Routledge, 1991, 1–13.

J. Morris and R. Imrie, *Transforming Buyer–Supplier Relations: Japanese Industrial Practices in a Western Context*, London, Macmillan, 1992.

T. Morris-Suzuki, 'Reshaping the international division of labour: Japanese manufacturing investment in South-East Asia', in J. Morris (ed.), *Japan and the Global Economy*, London, Routledge, 1991, 135–53.

M. Munday, *Japanese Manufacturing Investment in Wales*, Cardiff, University of Wales Press, 1990.

M. Munday, 'The financial consequences of linkages with Japanese manufacturers', *Management Accounting*, 68(7), 1990, 42–3.

M. Munday, 'Integrated materials management – beyond component quality', *Logistics Today*, 10(4), 1991, 27–35.

National Defence Counsel for Victims of Karoshi, *Karoshi: When the Corporate Warrior Dies*, Tokyo, Mado-Sha, 1990.

L. Naylor, 'Bringing home the lessons', *Personnel Management*, 16(3), 1984, 34–7.

The Observer, various issues.

K. Ohmae, *The Borderless World*, London, Collins, 1990.

N. Oliver and B. Wilkinson, *The Japanization of British Industry*, 2nd edn., Oxford, Blackwell, 1992.

T. Ozawa, 'International investment and industrial structure: new theoretical implications from the Japanese experience', *Oxford Economic Papers N.S.*, 31, 1970, 72–9.

T. Ozawa, 'Technical alliances of Japanese firms: an "Industrial Restructuring" account of the latest phase of capitalist development', Paper presented at the Symposium of New Technology, Technical Alliances and Social Innovations Within the Enterprise, Université du Quebec, Montreal, October 1992.

K. K. Pang and N. Oliver, 'Personnel strategy in eleven Japanese manufacturing companies in the UK', *Personnel Review*, 17(3), 1988, 16–21.

T. Pegge, 'UK management/union relations – Japanese style', Trent Polytechnic Business School, Open Lecture, 13 November 1984.

T. Pegge, 'Hitachi two years on', *Personnel Management*, October 1986, 42–7.

V. Pucik, 'Managing Japan's white-collar workers', *Euro-Asia Business Review*, 4(3), 1985, 16–21.

V. Pucik, M. Hanada and G. Fifield, *Management Culture and the Effectiveness of Local Executives and Japanese-Owned US Corporations*, New York, Egon Zehnder, 1989.

Regional Trends, 25, 1991.

W. Reitsperger, 'Japanese management: coping with British industrial relations', *Journal of Management Studies*, 23(1), 1986, 72–88.

J. E. Roemer, 'Japanese direct investment in manufacturing: some comparisons with the US pattern', *Quarterly Review of Economics and Business*, 16, 1976, 91–111.

M. Saso, *Women in the Japanese Workplace*, London, Hilary Shipman, 1989.

G. Sewell and B. Wilkinson, 'Someone to watch over me: surveillance, discipline and the just-in-time labour process', *Sociology*, 26(2), 1992, 271–89.

D. Simpson, 'Why are Welsh wages so low II?', *Welsh Economic Review*, 5(1), 1992.

J. Slaughter *'The team concept in the US auto industry'*, Paper presented to the Conference on the Japanization of British Industry, Cardiff Business School, 17–18 September 1987.

South Wales Echo, various issues.

The Times, various issues.

M. Trevor, *Toshiba's New British Company*, London, 1988.

Wales TUC, General Council, *Wales TUC and Inward Investment*, Positional paper approved by the Wales TUC General Council, 8 July 1987.

Welsh Affairs Committee, *Inward Investment into Wales and its Interaction with Regional and EEC Policies*. Minutes of Evidence 22.2.88 and First Report 14.12.88, London, HMSO.

Welsh Economic Trends, 1992.

Western Mail, various issues.

M. White, *The Japanese Overseas: Can They Go Home Again?*, Free Press, New York, 1988.

M. White and M. Trevor, *Under Japanese Management: The Experience of British Workers*, London, Heinemann, 1983.

P. Wickens, *The Road to Nissan*, London, Macmillan, 1987.

B. Wilkinson and N. Oliver, 'Power, control and the *Kanban*', *Journal of Management Studies*, 26(1), 1989, 47–58.

K. Williams, C. Haslam, J. Williams, A. Adcroft and S. Johal, *Factories or warehouses? Japanese manufacturing direct investment in Britain and the United States*. Occasional papers on Business Economy and Society, 6, London, Polytechnic of East London, 1992.

J. P. Womack, D. T. Jones and D. Roos, *The Machine that Changed the World: The Triumph of Lean Production*, New York, Rawson Macmillan, 1990.

S. Young, 'Scotland v Wales in the inward investment game', *Quarterly Economic Commentary*, 14(3), 1989, 59–63.

C. Yu and B. Wilkinson, *Pay and Appraisal in Japanese Companies in Britain*, Japanese Management Research Unit Working Paper No. 8, Cardiff Business School, UWCC, 1989.

Index